D1615525

SMOKE AND STEAM!

footplate memories of the G.N. and L.N.E.R.
in the 1920s

SMOKE AND STEAM!

footplate memories
of the G.N. and L.N.E.R. in the 1920s

Harold Bonnett

BRADFORD BARTON

This book is copyright under the Berne Convention; all rights reserved. No part may be reproduced, stored in a retrieval system, or transmitted in any form or means, electronic, mechanical, photocopying or otherwise, without the prior written permission of the publishers.

HERTFORDSHIRE
COUNTY LIBRARY
625.261
1054965

20 JUL 1982

ISBN 0 85153 395 7
copyright © Harold Bonnett 1981
set and printed by CTP Ltd for Top Link Ltd
for the publishers
D. BRADFORD BARTON LTD
Trethellan House · Truro · England

BD9473

CONTENTS

ILLUSTRATIONS

CHAPTER ONE

Getting to know the Great Northern

MY GRANDMOTHER, Maria Bonnett, remembered being taken as a small girl to see the first Great Northern train run through Barkston station in 1852. My father, William, when I was born in 1907, was a signalman at the North Junction box. Whatever influence these facts may have had upon my own choice of the railway as a lifetime's career, I do not really know, but some spark of enthusiasm without doubt was passed on into my blood.

This tiny glow was soon fanned into flame during my schooldays, simply because Barkston, situated on the G.N. part of the East Coast Route to Scotland, was one of the most wonderful places in the whole country for sights and sounds of a great and a proud railway at work. And it was not only that the main line was there, because the Lincoln and Boston branch also crossed the parish. If a make-weight was needed also we had the single line ironstone siding that crept up nearly a mile into the quarries under the Lincolnshire Edge. You can well imagine how, when the engine came to change the loaded wagons for empties, two or three boys, conscripted unwillingly for gleaning ears of barley in the harvest fields alongside this line, ran from protesting mothers to look at the grey-painted G.N. 0–6–0 as it puffed past on the other side of the hedge.

During the First World War even the German Naval Airship Service took a fleeting interest in our local railways. On 28th July 1916, Zeppelin L.13 aimed a string of bombs at a London-bound troop train that had been stopped for its protection against attack in a cutting at Hougham, the next station down the main line. The fully-lit train was spotted by the Zeppelin commander who followed it southwards from Newark, hoping that it would eventually stop in a large station where his bombs would find a worthwhile target. However, railwaymen farther north, hearing the airship tailing the train full of soldiers, wired this fact forward to signalmen. Cyril Blake, in Hougham box, stopped the train. Down came the bombs, thump, thump, thump, one after the other but fortunately all fell harmlessly in fields close to the main line and the troop train.

Shortly after the First World War ended in 1918, I landed myself in for a job on summer Saturdays tending about eight of John Rilett's milking cows on roadside grass verges. The best place to go was along the Station Road, leading to Marston. On either side of the railway bridge banks there was plenty of long grass for the cows, whilst I had a lovely day paid to be looking at trains . . .

The expresses to and from Hull, Leeds or Edinburgh all had their destinations shown on red-painted boards fixed under the roof edges of the coaches, G.N. fashion. Big Atlantic locomotives dashed along in fine style with these crack trains finished in varnished teak. In contrast with the power and speed of the express passenger engines, the little 0–6–0s on the goods trains seemed miserably underpowered or overloaded. There was a lay-by next to the South signalbox in which slow goods trains were held waiting a path forward over the four uphill miles to Grantham. What a tussle it was when drivers of some of these goods trains tried to pull out! Their engines used to creep at snail's pace, grunting and groaning as they strained at the heavy loads – usually coal. Often it was touch-and-go whether they got out at all. Not infrequently steam ran out over the first half mile, bringing the train to a stand with the need to set back into the lay-by.

What was known as the Link Line, which avoided Grantham for Nottingham to Boston side trains, also passed over the road a field's length west of the station. On those summer Saturdays of 1919–1921 there passed a constant stream of long excursion trains carrying trippers from Leicester, Derby and Nottingham to the Lincolnshire coastal resorts of Mablethorpe and Skegness. One train followed another in a constant procession towards the coast, each of them well-loaded with trippers. Some were headed by green-painted 4–4–0 passenger engines, but great resort was made on these specials to the latest type of G.N. 0–6–0 goods design. Whilst the 6′8″ wheeled 4–4–0s ambled along with some grace, the smaller-wheeled 0–6–0s, with their siderods bobbing up and down furiously, seemed chased and unhappy with this seaside work. These, of course, were the days before road charabancs became common and the railways had practically all the excursion traffic to resorts every where-around Britain.

It was at night-time, especially in winter, that the main line looked most spectacular. An older boy, Jack Millar, used to fetch copies of the *Nottingham Evening Post* off the down evening Parliamentary train. I sometimes went with him. Red and green signal lights showed the course of the line in the darkness. The signalman in the South box could be seen moving to and fro in front of his levers. Then, quite suddenly, a down or north-bound express would come out of the night with a tremendous earth-shaking clatter as it roared through the station. Heading it would be an Atlantic with its bright fire-flash lighting up the cab and throwing a glowing pattern of orange firelight on the underside of its trailing cloud of smoke and steam. What frightening, fiery, noisy devils those racing engines looked by night! Yet there stood the driver on the right side of his cab apparently unconcerned except about keeping his eyes upon the signals ahead.

The up or south-bound expresses had a special show of their own as they climbed the 1 in 200 grade. This climb made those big Atlantics fairly roar at their chimneys. And what a firework display they produced as their fierce exhausts threw out a constant stream of red-hot sparks high up into the night sky. Later on, of course, when these Atlantics were all fitted with superheaters, this meant the end of those free fireworks spectaculars.

The grass banks of the Jericho Woods cutting were scythe-mown at least once a year by the platelayers – a treatment that suited the wild strawberries which grew there. After school hours we village boys went there in June to pick the berries for home jam-making. Train spotting as such was not known then, but what marvellous summer evenings they were for us with trains racing past all the time. After starting from Grantham four miles up the line, the green Atlantics had got their trains going at around sixty miles an hour; how they used to sway about as they came cantering down the grade. It was during those formative years of youth that I made up my mind for certain that I wanted to be a locomotive man.

Meanwhile, I left school at 14 to work on John Rilett's seventy-acre farm, still keeping an eye of course on the passing trains. I remember in April 1922 that my boss and I were loading some barley straw that he had bought at the West Fields farm, a field away from Barkston station. I noticed a light engine coming up the line from the Doncaster direction. This green-painted locomotive was certainly a stranger to me, and very big it looked, too. As it clanked lightly through the station, I saw that it had the oddity of a hump-backed boiler, a massive side-windowed cab and six driving wheels. There had been hints in some newspapers that Gresley was building a masterpiece of an express engine for the G.N.R. At once I put two and two together – this was the promised Pacific, as indeed it was, No. 1470 *Great Northern*, on its first trial trip. Somehow or other I had the immediate feeling that the G.N.R. was going to have the best express passenger locomotives in Britain. No.1470 certainly looked and sounded like a winner.

In January 1923 the Great Northern became part of the newly-formed London & Northern Railway. However, in locomotive matters the influence of the old G.N.R. was to remain effective for many years.

Although I wanted to become an engine cleaner as soon as I could manage it, I had heard how difficult it was to get accepted. Wages and conditions were so good that competition was extremely keen. It was said that a record book was kept at Grantham Loco depot, in which the names of applicants were recorded; by hook or by crook, I had to get my name in that book.

If I ever did get this job as an engine cleaner, it meant spending several years on the work before I had a chance to become even a spare fireman. At the best I would be middle-aged before I became a driver, although I must say I did not hanker for the railway just to be, in the end, a driver. I was sure that my interest in steam engines was so great that I had no doubt at all but that I should enjoy every day spent working on them.

My father, as soon as he knew what I wanted to be, made an appointment for a Saturday morning interview at the 'loco' as it was called. We cycled into Grantham to the depot on the south-west side of the station. The yard was busy and noisy with engines of a great variety of classes, large and small, in green, black or grey liveries puffing up and down, whilst others stood either singly or in long rows. There was smoke and hissing steam everywhere. Drivers carrying oil cans, or firemen with lamps in their hands, passed to and fro along the sleeper or cinder paths. When we reached the end of the coal stage building, an elderly man wearing a bowler hat and polished black leather leggings – obviously a foreman of some kind – came out of a long low wooden office building. He directed us to the red-brick office of William A. L. Emerson, the Locomotive Depot Superintendent.

Very nervously, I knocked on the General Office door with its highly-polished brass letter-box plate and an equally well-shone door knob. We were asked inside. Sitting on a high stool was Harry Christopher, the chief clerk. He was a tallish heavily-built man, somewhat beetle-browed and with a bushy impressive moustache. On his nose rested a pair of gold rimmed spectacles, and the very least that you could say of him was that he had about him a marked air of clerical authority and importance.

After my father had explained our business, Mr. Christopher told a young clerk to bring the eyesight test card into the yard. Whilst I stood with my boot toes against a marked line on the forecourt, the clerk held the card against the office wall. Mr. Christopher, using a piece of cardboard to blank out alternate eyes, made sure that I could read the small letters on the last line but one. Then, back in the office, I was asked to pick out red, yellow and green colours among a mixed collection of worsted strands kept in a box in order to make sure that I was not colour blind.

My father and I were thereafter shown into Mr. Emerson's private office next door. He was a slightly built man, well-dressed in a smart suit of clothes and with a well-trimmed moustache. On his desk were a few papers, but what I noticed most were his highly-polished brass pen rack and paper weights. Around the walls hung a collection of large framed photographs of various classes of Great Northern locomotives.

Mr. Emerson spoke first to my father in a very pleasant and cultured voice. I knew at once that I had met my first gentleman of the railway. Turning to me he asked, "So you want to be an engine cleaner?" I think I just said, "Yes, please," or something like that before he went on to ask what standard I had reached at school. He then exchanged a few pleasantries of conversation on railway matters with my father, finishing up by saying, "We will put your boy's name down, Bonnett." Mr. Christopher was then called back in and told that I had been accepted.

The station at Barkston, my home town, looking south – a photograph taken on a winter day in or about 1950. It was here that Gresley's Mallard *began her world speed record run in 1938.*

[Author's Collection]

When we got back into the general office Mr. Christopher, reaching up to a rack over his desk, took down a reddish-brown leather bound book, so large that he needed both hands to lift it. It was, of course, *the* book into which the names of accepted applicants for cleaners' jobs were entered, and about which I had heard so much by hearsay. The chief clerk turned the pages until he came to the last entry. Then, very deliberately, he wrote down my name, address and date of birth. That done, he turned to my father and said, "We shall send for him when we want him. In any case that will not be before he is seventeen next February." His parting remark to me was, "Don't come here bothering us with enquiries about your chances of starting – you will be called in your turn!" As Mr. Christopher put the book back into the rack, he left me with the no uncertain impression that, by putting my name into it, he had conferred a great favour upon me. I agreed, and once outside the office door, I felt that I was walking on air. On John Rilett's farm I had earned 75p a week. As an engine cleaner on £1.80 a week, I was now going to be fairly rich.

CHAPTER TWO

Cleaning at Grantham

IT WAS ON A brand new Raleigh bicycle that I rode away from home on Monday 24th March 1924 in order to begin work at Grantham Loco. The steam hooter on the roof of the agricultural engineering works owned by Ruston & Hornsby sounded the 'five minutes-to-eight' warning to its scurrying workers before I was halfway through the town. I was going to be late! The tall chargeman cleaner, Charlie Torr saw me running up the path alongside the coal stage and punched my time card for me at exactly 8.00am. My face was red from the exertion and all he said was, "You'll have to do better than this, lad!"

At seventeen years and two months, I was the youngest of four new cleaners starting that day. Charlie Torr came into the cleaners' messroom and, mixing old and new hands together, arranged us into gangs of four. He gave a senior cleaner in each gang a pink stores order card on which was written the number of an engine, together with a list of the cleaning materials that could be drawn from the oil stores.

The storesman tossed two dozen once-washed khaki-coloured sponge cloths on to his tin-topped counter, took two pint-sized cans, and pulling at the handle of a pub barman's-type pump, splashed a pint of swob cleaning oil into each can. He next handed over four torch lamps and a pair of round red warning boards made of sheet steel. As we moved off to look for our engine, the old hands were clearly distinguished by the fact that they wore company's issue light blue overalls, lettered L.N.E.R. in red at the ends of the jacket collars, in contrast with the ordinary old clothing worn by the beginners. I sported an oversize signalman's blue serge jacket given to me by my father.

The gang began work by hanging the warning boards, lettered NOT TO BE MOVED, on the lamp brackets at either end of the engine – which in our case turned out to be an Atlantic. These boards warned shed shunt crews, or any other enginemen that cleaners were working on the engine; on no account must another engine be allowed to buffer up against it.

We then paired up, shared out the cleaning stuff, tossed a penny for choice of left or right side of engine, and dived into our work at once. The method was simple enough. One cleaner took a swob-soaked sponge cloth (swob oil was a mixture of paraffin and slightly heavier oil) and began on the boiler, whilst the other took the wheels. As no ladders were provided, it was something of a monkey climb scaling up the boiler barrel in order to get one's feet on the handrail about ten feet off the ground, but we were nimble enough to take no notice of that.

The swob-oiled wiper was rubbed over the whole surface in order to soften up the dirt, followed by a thorough wiping off with a clean sponge cloth. The transformation was immediate; paintwork that had been dull and lifeless before, soon shone with a lustre that gave sparkle to the whole engine. At once it took on a brighter and prouder look altogether. That was why engine cleaning, a dirty enough job in itself, was always quite rewarding in its results. One could certainly always see where one had been.

It was the wheels and lower parts that picked up the most dirt plus the oil splashes from the motion, but since they could be reached from ground level, they were the easiest parts to clean. Very early in the day I was told that it was 'a must' to clean round the backs of the wheel spokes, even though nobody ever saw this part of them. This was no leg-pull either, because the chargeman cleaner used to come round, take out a new sponge cloth and wipe it down the back of a few spokes. The slightest bit of missed dirt showed up on his cloth as a big sinful stain.

The tender and motionwork under the engine were cleaned last of all. Inside the shed it was dark on the red-painted 'underneaths' as we called them, so we had to use flare lamps – modelled on the lines of the bronze ones of ancient Rome. Our lamps, however, were made of tin and instead of burning sweet olive oil they had to manage with swob oil. The finger-thick white cotton wicks burned with an orange flame that ended in a pother of smelly smoke from which drifted away a stream of black balls of soot. This meant that a cleaner's lamp had to be placed so that the draught carried away the soot from his face. What a primitive and unhealthy form of illumination it was – yet we took it as just part of the game. Often one's lamp would fall accidently from the axlebox top or big end upon which it had been rested, leaving one in complete darkness and possibly with one's body wedged between the connecting rod and side frame.

The old piecework payment system had gone long before I started. But there was a time allowance arrangement that gave the chargeman cleaner a yardstick as to the amount of work he might expect from each cleaner. Eight hours was allowed for a small black 0–6–0 goods engine, complete; for an Atlantic it was twelve hours, whilst in the case of the three new Pacifics that attracted endless attention, no less than sixteen hours was allotted for the engine alone, plus an additional four hours for the tender. If an engine was particularly dirty, a 'plonker' as we called it, extra time would be allowed at the chargeman's discretion. Similarly, when an engine was booked to work a Royal train, or any other special working requiring a really smart 'knobbing-up', more time was granted accordingly.

The inside of the cab was not included in the cleaning of

an engine. Firemen on smaller locomotives had to clean their own cab fittings. On the bigger express engines such as the Atlantics or the Pacifics, the cabs (or fronts as they were always called) were cleaned and polished by caller-up cleaners in between their visits to call enginemen from their homes. This was so except on the night shift when one particular cleaner was detailed as the 'front rubber.' On the outside of it, a cab was a cab, but once you climbed up and went inside it, you were 'on the front.' This I think was an example of a word surviving from the pre-1880 days when Great Northern engines had no cabs as such to protect enginemen from wind and weather. The crews simply stood in front of the uncovered end of the boiler and firebox, and that to them was the 'front.'

During my first few weeks, I helped to clean a wide variety of engines, but the one that I liked more than any other was a mere 0–6–0 1911 goods engine, No.523, still wearing her wartime G.N. grey livery. I had always liked the good looks and purposeful grunts and clanks made by these superheated class "A" locomotives. Their highly perched boilers allowed one to see under the full length of the barrels. To me, the more that one saw of the boiler barrel of an engine, the more impressive and striking was the appearance. My enthusiasm was so keen that I scraped away a lot of old hard dirt from the edges of her wheel splashers and her makers brass plate was left shining quite brightly for a freight engine.

Of all the places in the Loco, none was so personal to the cleaners as their messroom. They went to it immediately after clocking on duty, then back to it for their one-hour meal break, and returned to it again about five minutes before going home. They seldom went into the messroom in between these times. If an engine was cleaned in less than the time allowed for it, the half hour or so that had been 'made' on the job was whiled away somewhere in the shed, rather than in the messroom where idlers could be caught quite easily, either by the chargeman cleaner, or by the

Running Foreman.

This messroom was actually the bricked-in space of an arch that formed part of the elevated coal stage building. It had a brown door, with the word CLEANERS painted on it in black letters. The inside walls were plain brick painted a dull brown, whilst the arched brick roof had no more than a coat of whitewash. A dozen or so coat pegs at the door end were the only wall fittings. For heating, there was a plain cast-iron fireplace, without oven or boiler. A piece of old rail, bent at either end, served as an unbreakable fender.

The strange thing was that, although engine cleaning was a filthy job at the best of times, there was neither a cold nor a hot water tap provided; neither was a kettle, making it impossible to make tea. The drivers and firemen, who had their rather better laid-out messroom next door, were allowed a one-gallon cast-iron kettle; but cleaners were not supposed to go into their room. However, on the day and afternoon shifts, those who wanted to brew tea for their meals usually managed to sneak boiling water by some means or other from the drivers' room adjoining. A special arrangement applied on the night shift when the two callers-up/cleaners were allowed to go into the drivers' room and make all the cleaners' tea shortly after midnight. Our tea cans were then left stewing on top of the stove until we went to our 1.0am meal. By that time, of course, as can be imagined, the tea was pretty black and over-stewed.

The only pieces of furniture in the messroom were two heavy tables with scrubbed tops, and half a dozen wooden forms to sit on. A shove-half-penny board, cut into the top of one table many years ago, was the one recreational feature in the entire room.

A big window filled the end of the room opposite the door, but its glass was always so grimy with coal dust and ash from the coaling and engine disposal road outside that it was a window in name only. A heavy iron grille protected the glass from the intermittent showers of coal that fell from the coaling tip above. Lighting was provided by a gas burner hung from the ceiling. Its unprotected mantle popped and popped all the time it was lit.

All new cleaners had to be initiated, a crossing-the-line ceremony that was always observed on the night shift. The night turn started at 12.5am on Monday mornings of all times. Each railwayman was guaranteed six weekly shifts of eight hours; but Sunday work did not count. Had we started before midnight on Sunday, we should have been entitled to another six shifts that week. As the railway wanted us to work only six nights in a week, we were booked 12.5am, and then doubled up with a second shift commencing at 9.0pm Monday night.

On my first Tuesday 1.0am mealtime, without any warning, an old hand jumped up, shouting "Below!" as he threw a sponge cloth at the gas mantle, smashing it to smithereens and putting the whole place into darkness. Two old hands previously-appointed rushed to the door as acting policemen lest anyone try to escape. Then a couple of self-styled 'judges' addressed themselves to one of the new hands, requesting whether he would like to sing a song, or have a dozen strokes with a belt across his bottom. He offered to sing, but since he did not sing very well, the 'judges' ruled that he must have a 'dozen'. Firmly held down by four hefty old hands flat on a table, he had his ration from a thick leather belt. However, since he did not make any particular struggle or protests, it was ruled that he liked it and must have another 'dozen'.

When my turn came Roy Mitchell said, "Ah! here's a farmer's boy from Barkston! How about singing 'The Farmer's Boy'?" Cross about it all, I refused to sing at all. Thereupon I was set upon, overpowered and well belted. But the judges ruled that I had resisted their wishes and must have another round. Quite obviously, one could not win at this long-established custom of rough fun.

After that things quietened down and I remember many happy middle-of-the-night meals in that room. Some of the lads who lived in Grantham lodgings frequently complained about their landladies and not without reason.

One night shift cleaner had a grouse that neither he nor his mate had been able to get off to bed the previous morning. It seemed that when they arrived home off their night shift around 6.15a.m., their landlady had given them breakfast. But she then blandly told them that two chorus girls from the local theatre, known to us at the Loco as the Gaff, were in their bed so they must wait until the girls came down. Apparently, after the cleaners had gone to work, a man from a travelling company had come round looking for a night's digs for some of his girls. Whether she had taken them in just to be obliging, or wanted to make a little extra money by double-letting the bed, was not known. What was considered the worst part of it all was that when the girls got up about eight o'clock, the landlady straight away made up the bed and told her two regular lodgers they could now go upstairs. "We had to get into the warm bed just as those girls got out of it, and after tarts like them!", said the poor fellow.

The chargeman/cleaner ate his meals sitting on a high stool at a little desk he used in a corner of the Running Foreman's office. It was rare that he ever came to the messroom at our mealtimes. Some of the top link main line firemen, however, were plain terrors to us on the night shift. They would fling open the door of our messroom, demanding, "Who is the front rubber on our engine?" Their trouble was that they considered the brass fittings or the inside of the cab on their Atlantic or perhaps a Pacific had not been properly done. The unfortunate front rubber would leave his meal to follow the irate fireman back to his engine in order to finish the cleaning to his satisfaction. Cecil Swingler, who fired to Joe Baines on Pacific No. 1476 *Royal Lancer*, was noted for these 'fetchings-out'. Cecil caught me at least once. "Look at this lot!" he bawled, pointing to several slightly oily patches on the green doors of the tender front tool boxes. "The swob has never been wiped off," he went on, "and I am not going to get it on my clothes." He certainly had half a case against me.

It was, of course, questionable whether these top link firemen had the right to drag a cleaner out so unceremoniously from his meal. But so much did we stand in awe of these self-important personages that we humble cleaners always went without a single word of protest. Mind you, the Pacifics were at that time kept in such splendid order that nobody wanted to be regarded as a nigger in the woodpile.

CHAPTER THREE

Some Grantham Locomotives

THERE WERE ABOUT fifty to sixty locomotives, all G.N. types, allocated to Grantham in the 1920s. Covered space for the necessary cleaning, boiler-washing and repairs was provided in two separate engine sheds, situated at opposite ends of the depot. Near to the station stood the Old Shed, built of red brick shortly after the G.N. laid its main line into the town in the early 1850s. In 1899 the Top Shed, with deeper pits and more working space between its four long roads, was added at the south end of the site, close to Springfield Road. As Grantham was mainly concerned with passenger working, half its stud of engines were 4–4–0, 4–4–2 or 4–6–2 types.

G.N. locomotives, originally contained in the number range 1 to 1770, had 3000 added to their numbers under the 1923 LNER grouping arrangements. This re-numbering, however, was carried out as the engines passed through Doncaster Plant for general repairs, so it was two or three years before all the numbers were actually corrected.

The oldest, and perhaps the most interesting of our engines, was 40-ton 0–6–0 saddle tank or 'Humpy' No. 3134A. Patrick Stirling built her at Doncaster in 1890, so she was already thirty-five years old. Not many alterations or additions had been made to her, for she remained domeless (Stirling did not believe in steam domes), had a tall conical brass safety-valve cover, rectangular wheel spokes and the small swept-back steel plate that Stirling thought was enough cab cover for his weather-hardened G.N. engine-men. The suffix A on her number indicated that there was another and newer engine also numbered 3134. Our engine was the 'A' or duplicate one of the two, the G.N. having quite a few such duplicate engines.

This venerable engine, like Cinderella, was kept at home doing all the odd jobs that other and grander sister engines doubtless regarded as below their station. They might set out for such fine towns as Leicester, Derby, Nottingham, Lincoln, Boston, Doncaster, York, or to King's Cross in London. Not so 3134A for, entirely within the confines of the shed outlet signal, she was kept busy, moving up and down seven days a week as the shed shunt engine. Some of her work was worth watching.

Sometimes, for example, an Atlantic had insufficient steam when the driver and fireman arrived on duty to work an express train, putting the Running Foreman into a bit of a stew. No. 3134A was brought to the rescue, coupled to the 4–4–2 in question and made to run her up and down the yard several times. The shed shunt fireman rode on the Atlantic so that he could place the reversing lever in the opposite direction to that actually travelled. This caused the pistons to force air into the boiler, building up a small pressure that could be used, in lieu of steam, to blow up the big engine's fire. Often this happened in the middle of the night when, by gas-light, these 'runnings-about' were something out of the ordinary. The sharp, gunshot style straight-up-in-the-air exhausts of 3134A were matched against a volume of dirty yellow-black smoke rolling heavily downwards from the chimney of the Atlantic. The noise of 3134A doing this job was something that must have awakened every light sleeper in the area.

You should also have seen our 'Humpy' when she took four or five loaded coal wagons up the ramp of the elevated coal stage! With the wagons in front of the smokebox, her driver set back some fifty yards or so on the level in order to get a flying start, then pulled the regulator wide open and went hell for leather at it. How the engine barked at her chimney and what a pillar of smoke and steam she threw up into the sky! But the run called for fine judgement. Any nervous driver who shut off steam seconds too soon, fearing that he might knock out the other end of the coal stage, was brought to a stand with his engine still a wagon length or two short of the entrance. Then, nothing on earth would induce 3134A to re-start, so down the whole lot had to come and the run had to begin all over again.

Of the other three or four Humpies that shunted the up and down goods yards, the two ex-Metropolitan tankies on the passenger shunts, or the assortment of ageing Class B 0–6–0 goods engines that looked after the branch line freight work, there is nothing in particular to report. One, I recall was 0–6–0 No. 3850 built in 1892 by Stirling, but improved by the substitution of a larger boiler with a dome on it.

In 1896, Henry A. Ivatt had succeeded Stirling as the Locomotive Engineer at Doncaster, so it was natural to find that we had more Ivatt-designed locomotives than any others at Grantham in 1924. About half-a-dozen of his 4–4–0 W Class provided power for the passenger services on the Leicester, Nottingham, Lincoln and Boston branches. Two of them were Nos. 4338 and 4339 which, like the majority of their hundred or so sisters, were wet steamers with slide-valve steam distribution. Now, in all the long locomotive history of the old G.N., these were the only express passenger engines that were mediocre performers and one will not find their exploits recorded anywhere in railway history. Their great fault was that they were shy steamers; mind you, some enginemen averred that even when they had only about 120lb of steam, instead of their full 175lb working pressure, they could still run fast – provided, that is, that the load behind them was not too heavy. Ivatt, who had designed these engines with a view to giving his inherited enginemen freedom from worry about steam shortages on the road, was really concerned about the result. Although, as time went on, he provided bigger boilers and even a superheated version, there was no improvement.

From 4–4–0s Ivatt had turned to the Atlantic type, for in 1898 he built No. 990 *Henry Oakley*. Its cylinder and motion work was modelled upon a 4–4–2 of the Atlantic Coast Lines Railroad in the U.S.A. and it was from the same source that the type name Atlantic was introduced into Britain. Incidentally, No. 990, the first British Atlantic was sent to Grantham for her early proving trials whilst Ivatt went back to America for further ideas. When he returned, he found that the depot superintendent at Grantham, a disbeliever in engines that drove off the rear driving axle, had soft-pedalled with the trials. He was transferred to York shed in what was really a down-grading.

The Klondykes, as these new Atlantics were dubbed by the men, were a big improvement as regards pulling and running power for steam when on the fastest and heaviest turns. Disappointed a second time, Ivatt turned his thoughts to a boiler of outsize proportions. It was in 1902 that this large Atlantic No.251 appeared with what looked like a top heavy boiler on which the firebox had a wide Wootton firegrate.

Between 1902 and 1911 ninety-three of these large Atlantics were built at Doncaster (Nos.251, 272–301, 1400–1461; old GN numbering), and in 1924 we had some twenty-five of them at Grantham. Now the extraordinary thing was that one never heard a wrong word said about these engines. In fact, everybody praised them, a sure sign that they must have been good at their work. Indeed, one heard tales of how, during the 1914–1918 War, when engine power was at a premium, it had been known for Atlantics to bring 600-ton trains out of King's Cross, and had kept time with them, too. What had really turned them into first class locomotives was the fitting, from about 1910 onwards, of superheaters. The hotting-up of steam from the usual 380 °F to around 500 °F produced an effect where a greater volume of steam was generated for each pound of coal burnt, and that steam did more work simply because it was resistant to condensation. It was after this superheating that the Atlantics excelled as galloping iron greyhounds on the old Great Northern. During the mid-1920s there was a reporter on the staff of the *Daily Express* who gave an account of all their latest outstanding performances, especially with the Harrogate Pullman trains. But the days of Atlantics in premier place were already over, for the sun was rising on the no-less glorious day of the Pacific.

The really promising showpieces at Grantham in 1924 were the three Gresley Pacifics built the previous year. We had No. 1476 *Royal Lancer*, No. 1479 *Robert the Devil* and No. 1480 *Enterprise*. It is interesting now to reflect that these cost only £7,500 apiece to build. They formed part of a batch of twelve such 4–6–2s authorised by the G.N. Board of Directors before the 1923 Grouping. What big engines they looked in comparison with the Atlantics! They were, in fact, so high above the rail that the smoke jacks on No. 1 Road in the Top Shed had to be specially raised in order to give their cab tops clearance. Two crews were allocated to each Pacific for the purpose of sharing the daily 376-mile round trips: Grantham-London-York-Grantham. The London crew ran 210 miles whilst the York one involved only 166 miles.

These Pacific Link enginemen thought that they were the cat's whiskers, all coming to work very smart in well-washed and well-ironed company-issue blue jean overalls plus caps with soft tops. Drivers like Joe Baines or Bob Chatwin who shared *Royal Lancer* also came to work in boots as brightly polished as those of the General Manager at King's Cross.

Nor must the cleaners be overlooked. Eight of them, picked for the job, were arranged in two shifts, to clean only the three Pacifics.

The man from whose brain the design of the Pacifics had

originated was Herbert Nigel Gresley, who in 1936 was knighted. He came from the Lancashire & Yorkshire to the G.N. in 1905 to become Carriage & Wagon Superintendent at Doncaster. In 1911 he succeeded Ivatt as the Locomotive Engineer at the early age of 35, to the chagrin of some senior engineers who were overlooked for this important post.

Like almost every other engineer, Gresley had the aim of creating a bigger and better express locomotive than his predecessors. At first he toyed with the idea of a big four-cylinder machine but his trials with Atlantic No.279, modified with four cylinders and Walschaerts valve gear, were disappointing. A complete switch was then made to a three-cylinder arrangement that was subsequently proved practicable with the ten G.N. mixed traffic 2–6–0s (Nos.1000–1009), the first of which appeared in 1920.

Strange though it may seem, Gresley, following Ivatt's footsteps before him, went to the U.S.A. and there obtained some of his best ideas. The Pennsylvania Railroad had some very famous K4 class Pacifics, with boilers that steamed splendidly. The telling feature was that they were widest with most water where the firebox heat was more intense, i.e. at the bulge where the firebox was joined to the boiler barrel. Inside this swollen end section of the boiler was a forward open extension of the firebox space, known as the combustion chamber. It was the answer to efficient combustion and rapid conduction of heat into the boiler water. This style of boiler was copied for the G.N.R.

When Gresley turned out 4–6–2 No.1470 in 1922, he undoubtedly set the seal on the basic principles of express passenger locomotive design on the East Coast Route until the end of steam traction in the mid-1960s. The Pennsy boiler, coupled with three cylinders, reigned supreme for 45 years – no mean achievement!

Of Gresley personally, I never remember hearing any driver or fireman say they had seen him. It is said that he never drove any of his own locomotives, nor those of any

G.N. 4–4–0 No.4339, a sister of 'W' class Nos.4301, 4346 and 4399, was one of the few superheated engines of this class; photographed at King's Cross.

[C.R.L. Coles]

No.1165, one of the Great Central four-cylinder engines that failed to beat our G.N. Atlantics on the Pullman trains.
[Author's Collection]

other engineer. Whilst Ivatt had got around quite a bit amongst his enginemen, even to the chairing of meetings in pre-trade union days when the enginemen were requesting improved pay and conditions, Gresley was more aloof. At the Doncaster Plant, however, the latter was held in great respect and some awe. His immediate subordinates knew him as The Great White Chief, for if those close to him were discovered doing things without his knowledge, he was quick to put them in their places with the sharp remark, 'I am in charge here!' Even in relationships with his Board of Directors, he never suffered fools gladly, for he could be mildly insolent in his correspondence with some of them.

At Grantham, the Pacific crews, like those at Doncaster and King's Cross, had taken kindly to their new engines. The cabs were roomy and comfortable, whilst the pitch and roll of the Atlantics' riding was also eliminated. Drivers at once found that they had ample power—at last the GN Section had an express engine absolutely boss of its job. The firemen didn't mind the fact that the engines did burn quite a bit of coal, because the boilers steamed beautifully. But for all their good points, initially these Pacifics had their faults.

After they had run about 20,000 miles, irregular exhaust beats were noted by drivers who began to book 'Valves require re-setting' on the daily repair sheets. Fitter Jack Peacock, a roundish quiet type of chap, was our valve-setting expert at Grantham, but what a time he had over this problem! What happened was that the engine would be stopped from running, put at the top of No. 1 shed road and all the valve chambers opened out in order the settings might be checked for accuracy. This was done time and time again. Sometimes three or four of us cleaners were sent to help pinchbar the heavy engine up or down a few yards in each direction whilst the positions of the three piston valves were checked.

I remember on one occasion Jack Peacock looking completely puzzled, along with Bob Rawden, the fitters' foreman. Rawden would take out his pince-nez reading glasses, perch them upon his nose and, aided with an electric hand torch, peer into the dark recess of a valve chamber. All seemed spot-on to him. Released for work again, the Pacific was due for the 5.18pm to King's Cross the same day. But as Peacock and his mate stood outside the side door of the shed to listen, to their dismay the exhaust beats of the London-bound engine were chuff-er – bang – chuff with the same irregularity as before.

Gresley's staff from Doncaster had to be brought in to solve this one. It was found that as soon as any appreciable wear had taken place in the bearings of the two-to-one valve gear levers, the setting of the middle valve was thrown out. Modification of the bearings in the levers cured the worst of the trouble, but it has to be said that to the end of their days, all Gresley three-cylinder engines retained that peculiar exhaust note. The heart of the trouble with the middle valve, of course, lay in the conjugated valve gear, where by means of levers linking the two outside valve rods with the middle one, two sets of gear were made to operate three valves. Gresley believed in this brain-child of his, but his successor in 1943, Herbert Thompson, abandoned it for new building, preferring to install a third set of valve gear for the middle valve.

CHAPTER FOUR

Coaling and a visit by a G.W.R. 'Castle'

IT WAS THE custom to use cleaners for relief purposes whenever any of the shed labourers were off sick or on holiday. The worst thing that could happen was to find oneself booked in place of the nobbler on the coal stage. During my spell of cleaning I had two such weeks, one night shift and one afternoon shift during very hot weather in July 1924.

The floor of the stage was about four feet higher than the cab tops of the engines, so that coal, in 10cwt two-wheeled iron tubs, could be tipped into their tenders below. And what a filthy dirty place it was, coal dust everywhere and lumps of coal littered all over the iron-plated floor! Two coalmen on each shift shared the heavy job of shovelling coal out of the wagons lettered G. LOCO N. into the tubs and tipping it over the two chutes, one at either end of the stage.

As each engine returned after the day's work, it was run on to what was called the ashpit road. After the fire and smokebox ash had been thrown out, the shed shunt or disposal crews moved the engine ahead under the coal stage. This was where the nobbler came in, for he had first to start filling the tender tank with water then as each tub was tipped, crack in half all the big lumps of coal. This was done with a fireman's long-handled hammer that had a pick point on one side and a striking head on the other. On Atlantics or Pacifics one also had the additional task of stacking bigger lumps of coal upright around the top edges of the tender. The lump-breaking precluded a fireman having any difficulty on the road with a large piece of coal possibly getting wedged in the shovelling hole, whilst the 'side-lumping' allowed more coal to be loaded on the tender, and at the same time prevented any from dropping off accidentally whilst the engine was working a train. It did happen occasionally, of course, that a big piece of coal slid off at speed – to smash up like an exploding bomb on some station platform, or with the possibility of hitting a lineside platelayer on the head. So, nobbling was a convict-style hard labour job, but it also carried certain responsibilities. The joke of it, too, was that although the shed labourer normally employed as a nobbler was paid £2.40 a week, unless a cleaner was eighteen years of age he was not paid the higher rate; but he was expected to do the job every bit as well as a man . . . . Alas, I was seventeen!

My first shift, 10.0pm to 6.0am, was a rough and unforgettable one. From the moment of starting – and no time was lost in doing so – there was not a slack minute until around 2.0am for we were right in the middle of the summer passenger season. In addition to the branch line locomotives that were coming home for the night, one after the other express passenger engines from the regular and extra main line trains piled up in a queue waiting for water and coal. Additionally, King's Cross crews who wanted topping up with coal before they returned home came in as extras. They were allowed to jump the existing queue by setting back on to the head of it under the south-end coaling chute.

Some Atlantics and the one Pacific we had passed that night had practically empty tenders. These engines were always loaded with the very best coal, which came from Grimethorpe colliery near Barnsley; it usually came in massive pieces, very hard to crack. It also broke with sharp edges that, unless one took great care, could cut fingers like a knife. Walking about on it, too, was rough on boots, for it slashed the leather to pieces in no time. Whilst an Atlantic might take four tons of coal, the huge gaping almost-empty tender to a Pacific that had last taken coal at King's Cross before setting out with 'The Flying Scotsman' through to York and then back to Grantham, wanted as much as seven tons. As you may imagine, there were plenty of lumps to crack in that amount of coal.

About 2.0am the coalmen and I stopped for our meal which we ate in the little wooden cabin standing at the north end of the stage. This, too, was smothered in coal dust, but we were all used to that. Some Grimethorpe best steam coal soon boiled our tea water in a kettle standing on the guard's van-type of free-standing cast-iron stove. Unless you have ever done a coal stage shift, you won't really know how wonderful a cup of tea can taste in the middle of the night!

My second week was on the 2.0pm to 10.0pm afternoon turn. One day, as I was cycling home from work, Canon Gilbert George Walker, the Barkston rector, had a quip at me for having chosen a dirty job. "My boy", he said "you're working at the wrong end of the train. You should be a guard wearing a gold-braided uniform, with the ladies coming up to you asking if you would see their daughters safely out of the train at their destinations – and handing you half-a-crown!" What he would have said had he known I was, that week, a mere relief coal cracker, I do not know . . . .

⋆ ⋆ ⋆

That week I learned a little about former Great Central express passenger locomotives. When the L.N.E.R. was formed in 1923, control of the Locomotive Running Department went to the old G.C.R. W.G.P.McClure became Locomotive Running Superintendent, with offices at Liverpool Street station. Now, at last – or so they thought –

there is an opportunity to show what G.C. express engines could do on the built-for-speed Great Northern Main line. Several of the big Robinson-designed 1921 green-painted Lord Faringdon class were moved over to King's Cross depot. These noisy machines carried such names as *Lord Stuart of Wortley* or *Valour*, the last-mentioned, of course,

Kings Cross driver Pibworth with No.4475 Flying Fox *at Grantham coal stage, 1924. Note 'Humpy' No.3134A at rear. [Author's Collection]*

being the G.C. war memorial engine. Each afternoon that I was at the coal stage, one of these G.C.R. 4–6–0s came down in the hands of Cockneys to take on coal and water before returning to London. The tender was well down for coal, although the 4–6–0 had run only the 105 miles from King's Cross. I recall the fireman was a slightly-built pale-faced chap in his thirties, and on each occasion he was busy occupied shovelling clinker out of the firebox. It was obvious that this engine, whatever other merits like sturdy construction, free steaming or good riding it may have possessed, was a heavy coal burner. To my surprise, on the Saturday evening, that fireman reached up to me on the coal of his tender and handed me a two shilling piece – quite a sum in those days.

After the G.C. 4–6–0s had had a go, some G.C. Director class 4–4–0s came over to try their paces, principally on the Harrogate Pullmans. But neither of these competitors from the Great Central picked up any laurels. Very soon they went back home, leaving our G.N. Atlantics free to revel for years to come on the Pullmans, which they raced along with their accustomed ease.

For years the G.W.R. and the Great Northern considered themselves as having the best express passenger locomotives. In 1925, it was agreed to test Gresley's Pacifics against C. B. Collett's very successful Castle class 4–6–0s on both L.N.E. and G.W. tracks.

As is now well-known, No.4079 *Pendennis Castle* came over to King's Cross depot in April 1925, in order to run against our Pacific No.2545 *Diamond Jubilee* allocated to Doncaster. At the same time King's Cross Pacific No.4474 *Victor Wild* went over to Old Oak Common depot to compete with No.4071 *Caldicot Castle* on Paddington to Plymouth trains.

Early one afternoon, *Pendennis Castle*, making a preliminary run, came into Grantham Loco yard. Naturally all the cleaners, as well as enginemen and other shed staff, were very interested in the forthcoming trials. So, as soon as news came that 4079 was actually in the yard, the chargeman cleaner let our gang go down to the 70′ turntable at the north end, where the G.W. engine was standing. My immediate impression was that this was a smaller and more sharply outlined engine than our Pacifics. Her main feature was the Belpaire firebox with its broad flat top and narrow firegrate tucked between the side frames, in direct contrast with the round narrow firebox top and wide firegrate of a Pacific. This Castle, too, made the Pacifics appear slightly top heavy and outsize. In livery, the 4–6–0 was painted a dark olive green, with black wheels, but I liked the apple green of our Pacifics quite as well.

A G.W. locomotive inspector was riding with the driver and fireman and all three of them were most obliging in allowing us to climb up into the cab. Actually, I had expected that we should be kept at arm's length. The firebox door was open, showing the fire built up level with the bottom ring of the firehole – a big fire by our standards and one that we should expect soon to have the safety valves blowing off . . . But everything seemed under quiet and proper control. The burning lumps of coal on top of the firebed looked like swollen or burst-open cauliflowers and I formed the impression that the engine was burning Welsh coal. However, according to all the records that I have since read, the G.W. Castle on these trials burnt only Yorkshire coal whilst on the L.N.E.R. I did, however, see the G.W. fireman do something that none of our men ever did, and that was to let the ash out of the firebars by taking a long pricker with a turned-up prong to run through the bars from the under, or ashpan side. Invariably L.N.E.R. firemen poked their fires only through the firehole in the cab.

When *Pendennis Castle* moved, she was smart in her action, with an easy and brisk exhaust beat. Her crew appeared quite unconcerned and relaxed and it was obvious that during their first run down from King's Cross, neither the weight of the train, nor any of the long gradients had worried them at all. Whilst most of the cleaners, like myself, thought that this engine would give a good account of herself, the pride that we had for our own Pacifics encouraged us to think that when the measured trials took place, ours would show this 'Wessy' how to run.

During the first week of the trials, I was on the night shift. Towards the end of that week both No.2545 and 4079 were put on the 4.24am Doncaster-London fast express which ran non-stop through Grantham at 5.20am. The mornings were now getting light, so we should have a grandstand view of the passing trains.

On Friday morning, 25th April, our *Diamond Jubilee* worked the train. The main line was about 150 yards away from the Top Shed, and five or six of us cleaners had a clear view as we looked from the cab of an engine standing in the Coronation Road, between two coal stacks. The up main line signals beside the Grantham Yard signalbox stood out clearly against the morning sky as we watched. At last, a few minutes before passing time, the signal arm fell into the down position. Then, dead on time, No.2545 came roaring through the station, pulling a long train. But, although she was on time, it was clear for all to hear that she was being worked hard by her driver. "Still", I thought, "She has made it, and was on time!"

On the Saturday morning there was an even more excited atmosphere, for now the 'Wessy' was on her first measured run up from Doncaster to London. How was she going to shape? I confess I kept hoping that the burning of Yorkshire coal would be her undoing. We again went to watch the course. At about a quarter past five, somebody said "The board's off!" Soon afterwards, we heard the rumble of the train coming through the station, although there were still five minutes to go before passing time. Over the tops of the wagons in the down goods yard I saw *Pendennis Castle* burst into view as she headed her train in a swift dashing style. The sound of her chimney exhaust was not much more than a whisper. "Some engine!", I thought, "Five minutes early, and going like that!" The 4–6–0 and its train slipped away under the Great North Road Bridge to disappear southwards on the long climb up to Stoke Summit. How that Great Western crew must have been bursting with hidden pride that morning!

Having seen and heard that impressive performance it was, to me, a foregone conclusion that the G.W. engine was going to beat us. During the following week, both engines continued their comparative trials, working the same 500ton train on alternate days.

These trials were spoken of as friendly locomotive exchanges; but I would go one further and say that they were undertaken in a gentlemanly spirit. For although the G.W. engines gave a decidedly better performance on either line, the Great Western authorities were too kind hearted to think of claiming that they were the winners. The plain facts were stated, but little more. Mind you, there were plenty of G.W. fans who gloried in the result – even today, one can meet them with the smile of victory still on their faces. The two Swindon-built Castles burnt about 6lb of coal less per mile, whether Welsh or Yorkshire, than the Doncaster-built Pacifics. The trials were a complete triumph for the Great Western and there was not the slightest doubt, but that the best engines had won.

In 1924, the L.N.E.R. made the Gresley 4–6–2 their standard express passenger locomotive. Shortly afterwards, five of the new Doncaster-built Pacifics came to Grantham. These were No.2547 *Doncaster*, No.2548 *Galtee More*, No.2549 *Persimmon*, No.2550 *Blink Bonny*, and No.2551 *Prince Palatine*. As the loading gauge on main line sections off the old G.N.R. was more restrictive, it had been necessary to cut down the height of the new engine's chimneys, domes, safety valves and cab roof. Furthermore, the front buffer plates of the G.N.-built Pacifics had been rectangular, but now a bite had been taken out of the bottom corners to conform to N.E. practice that prevented any risk of knocking out the coping stones of station platforms.

After the arrival of these new engines, I found myself cleaning mostly Pacific types, for the Atlantics had been superseded on many more of the main line expresses. As may be imagined, all the Pacific drivers expected that we should make a particularly good job of cleaning their charges. Joe Baines, the roundish, short-necked and peppery driver of *Royal Lancer* was, in particular, a terror to us at times, for he found fault wherever he could. Fortunately, Bob Chatwin, who shared *Royal Lancer* with Joe, was a quieter type of driver altogether. One summer's afternoon, when Joe came in a bad temper to work the 5.18pm to King's Cross, and apparently could find no small mechanical fault with which to plague the fitting staff, he turned on us. Spotting a smear on a valve rod of the Walschaerts gear, he swung round with his oil can at the end of his outstretched arm, flinging a stream of oil in a wide arc from the end of its spout. As he looked at the nearest cleaner, with a glare on his face, he bawled out, "Wipe that shodding dirt off!" Joe never swore,

Slide-valve Atlantic No.3281 on the turntable at Grantham in the 1930s.
[T.G. Hepburn]

but always mispronounced his favourite expression of sodding.

Supervision of our cleaning work, of course, was entirely in the hands of the shift chargeman cleaner. Jack Berridge, a short slightly bandy-legged man of about fifty, was the one whom most cleaners liked best. In the discharge of his duties to the railway company, he was conscientious to the extent that he was often a real worrier, especially on the Sunday afternoons when he was occasionally booked-in to look after the whole depot. So far as we cleaners were concerned, he saw to it that we did not skimp our work and, indeed, he frequently made us improve on our efforts, or took us back to wipe off some dirt from an engine we had just left. But Jack was absolutely fair and straightforward in all his dealings with us. This won him the ungrudging respect he deserved. Any of his cleaners would have needed to commit a really bad offence against the railway rules before Jack reported him to the Running Foreman, for in many ways he stood as our guardian angel between us and higher authority.

The Running Foremen didn't bother us a lot, except one new foreman who moved from Peterborough to Grantham about a year after I started work. From the start he took the worst possible interest in us. He was out to catch cleaners idling time and his method was not without merit. Wearing rubber-soled and -heeled boots, he used to steal up the shed walkways listening for muffled conversations, particularly between say four and five o'clock in the early mornings when the night shift lads felt the most tired. As soon as he suspected a resting group inside an engine cab, with the agility of a cat, he bounded up the steps and grabbed the two nearest cleaners by their coat collars. As the rest of the bunch threw themselves out of the opposite side cab door, our 'cat burglar' foreman tried to recognise as many faces as he could. The two who had been 'collared' were marched to the time office and booked off duty for the rest of the shift. That done, he found the chargeman cleaner and sent him out to bring in those whose faces he had, as best he could, attached names to. Where recognition was certain, they were also sent home without pay; whilst the doubtful cases got a good ticking off with a warning about the future. They were lively times and no mistake.

In spite of all the ups and downs of the supervision from various quarters, all the cleaners on Pacifics took a great pride in their work. The huge engines were kept very clean and well turned out. As with all G.N. locomotives, there was nothing like the amount of ornamental copper and brass found on Great Western engines, or even on the Great Eastern Section express passenger types. But we did make the green paintwork glisten, and we polished the steelwork until it shone like silver. The occasional bits of brass or copper, such as the oil boxes, oil pipes, maker's plate or the great curved nameplates, were also beautifully polished.

How lovely those Pacifics looked as, with steam hissing sharply from their cylinder water cocks, they rolled majestically away from the Top Shed to work an express. We used to stand and watch them pull away, admiring every inch of them. Although our work was dirty, we had the immense satisfaction of knowing that it gave life and lustre to those magnificent Gresley Pacifics of the London & North Eastern Railway. I must say that I thoroughly enjoyed my days as an engine cleaner, although such work would scarcely be socially acceptable to-day.

The summer of 1925 was a fairly busy one for the N.E.R. The British Empire Exhibition was in its second year at Wembley and numerous extra passenger trains were run to London in connection with it. It was much to my surprise when in September I was told that I should be examined for promotion to passed cleaner on Monday, 5th October. In those days, the railway did not do much in the way of staff training, for it was mostly a matter of self education at all levels of footplate work. What we used to do was buy books such as "From Cleaning to Driving" and, at the same time, discuss locomotive matters among ourselves or with the more experienced firemen. The Company did, of course, do something by way of encouragement to help the voluntary Enginemen's Mutual Improvement Classes, by providing a small wooden hut that could be used, mainly on Sunday mornings, for lectures.

On my examination day, I had started work on the 12.5am night shift along with four or five others. Inspector Allen of New England caught the first train from Peterborough and was ready to examine us at 8.0am. We each had to fill in a questionnaire, with five questions such as, 'How would you test the level of water in a boiler?; What would you do if you noticed an obstruction on the line?; What is a distant signal, and what is it used for?'; and so on. A few oral questions were then put to each candidate separately. Finally, we were all told that we had passed this first stage, and that a 'trial' trip as a fireman would be arranged for each of us as soon as possible. Once again I went home feeling pleased with myself. The prospect of becoming a spare fireman opened out an entirely new world to any plain engine cleaner.

CHAPTER FIVE

First Firing Turns

THE 9.5AM GRANTHAM to Bourne slow, or pick-up goods, was the one selected to give trial trips to cleaners passing out as spare firemen. Bowler-hatted Inspector Allen accompanied me on 10th November 1925, a fine, clear day for the time of year as I recall. Walter Ledger, a man in his sixties, who walked with a decided limp and did nothing but branch line freight work, was my driver. Our engine was No.4155, an Ivatt Class B 0–6–0. Walter's regular fireman had got it ready for me to climb up into the cab in the down goods yard. The fittings had been polished, the floorboards nicely swept clean and everything was in apple pie order.

When the signal from the yard out on the main line fell into the 'off' position, I looked back down the twenty or so wagons, and saw that the guard was leaning out of his brake van with his arm outstretched as the indication that he was ready to go. "Right away," I called out to driver Ledger, who pushed the reversing lever into the forward position before tugging at the long horizontal regulator handle. No.4155 budged forwards slightly, gave her first slow puff, then another and another as we started on our way.

Inspector Allen reminded me that I should again look back to the guard. The latter could be seen again holding his arm as required by the rule book to indicate that the whole train was moving along intact. "Don't put any coal on yet," said the Inspector. "Just keep a good look-out, back and front, until we are out on the main line."

As we went jogging along towards Barrowby Road signalbox, my first impression was that the rotating motion, especially the big ends, knocked and banged in a harder-hitting fashion than I had expected. However, since nobody else took any notice or made any comment, it was obvious this was the normal behaviour of one of these 0–6–0s at work. Half a mile out of Grantham, I put half a dozen shovelfuls of broken coal on to the fire. G.N. engines, with their hinged flaps inside the oval firehole door, were tricky enough to fire, simply because there was not much space to get the coal through under the flaps. There was certainly no room for larger lumps and, indeed, for beginners it was all too easy to spill half or all a charge of coal on to the cab floor. "Now that you have fired up," said the inspector, "it is your duty to help your driver by keeping a constant look-out."

We ran into Peasecliffe Tunnel. All the engine noises sounded louder, whilst the firelight played a reddish moving pattern on our smoke under the tunnel roof. The water level in the boiler had now dropped an inch or so down the two round glass tube water gauges so, somewhat apprehensively, I turned to the boiler feed-water injector on my side of the firebox faceplate. Injectors could be temperamental, so I feared the worst as, after pushing down the cold water handle, I turned the brass wheel of the steam cock. However, with but one little adjusting wriggle of the water handle, that injector smartly went into action without littering more than a few spots of water from the injector overflow pipe fixed below the bottom step of the cab.

On we went down through the Jericho Woods cutting where I had picked wild strawberries, then at Barkston South Junction signalbox we turned away eastwards on to the Boston branch. Soon thereafter we were passing the East signalbox where my father happened to be working on the morning shift.

At Honington station we did our first bit of shunting, for there were several wagons to set down and a few to pick up. For most of the time the guard, as well as the porter helping him to shunt, were on my side of the engine. With the inspector watching me carefully all the time, like a car driving test examiner, I had to relay correctly all the shunting hand signals to driver Ledger. After that we jogged on to Ancaster for another short spell of shunting. My fifteen miles of a trial trip ended about half past ten when we arrived at Sleaford. Another cleaner who was to be tested over the Sleaford to Bourne single line now got on to the footplate. Inspector Allen told me that he would pass me and that I could go back to Grantham Loco. Once again I was jubilant. Cleaning pay was 30 pence a day, but for firing it was the then fabulous sum of 45 pence a day.

Ten days later, whilst cleaning an engine around 1.0am in the morning, my second firing turn came quite unexpectedly. Strangely enough, I was a fireman without a driver; Running Foreman Bill Richardson had used up all his spare drivers on relief work. There was a queue of engines awaiting disposal on the ashpit and he had to do something about it. He told me to 'put away' or dispose of as many engines as I could on my own. The shed shunt crew were there to move the engines about as required, but I was to bang into the disposal work.

The ashpit work was extremely hard and trying. Most fireboxes, expecially those on the Atlantics, had up to a foot or so of clinker and half-burnt cinders in them. All this had to be taken out with a clinker shovel sporting an eight-foot handle that had a knack of getting entangled with fittings on the tender front as one drew the loaded shovelfuls out of the firehole. There was not much space either to throw the clinker out of the cab door space on to the ground. When it is said that the clinker was red-hot, often in large lumps that had to be broken up before they could pass through the firehole door, and that the iron handle of the shovel became too hot to touch without using an old sponge cloth, the rigours of the job will be appreciated. Furthermore, the shovel blade soon became white-hot and curled up at the business end, making it impossible to push into the clinker. The remedy for this was to do your own blacksmithing by beating the white hot blade flat with a fireman's hand hammer before slaking it under the injector cold water overflow pipe, and beginning again. On an engine that had a very big fire to come out, the shovel end might have to be beaten flat two or three times.

Emptying the smokeboxes, however, was not much of a job. One just opened the door at the front of the smokebox and, using the fireman's shovel, chucked out the hundredweight or so of fine black cinder and ash. Once the engine got up to the coal stage, the sand boxes were filled from spouted buckets whilst there was now a pit under the engine for raking ash out of the ashpan. What a 'fires of hell' place this was at night!

That night I nearly blotted my copy book, for I let an Atlantic get away from me with enough force to give a W class 4–4–0 a real smack. This little engine was half spent of steam so that the shed shunt fireman on it could not move up for coal. He asked me to give him a start. I blew up the vacuum brake to twenty-one inches on both needles, the correct vacuum, before opening the regulator. The engine wouldn't go forwards, so I flung back the reversing lever into back gear, with immediate response. Back went the lever into fore gear and, in an instant, my Atlantic shot forward. Although I reached over and closed the regulator with a sharp snap, and slammed down the vacuum brake handle it was too late – we hit the 4–4–0 in front with a resounding bump, knocking her two lengths forward. Both the shed shunt driver and foreman Richardson had heard the hit-up, but after assuring themselves that no buffer beams were bent, they went away without saying a word to me, nor did I hear any more about it. But the incident taught me a lesson.

Early in February I was taken off cleaning to go with passed fireman George Bednall who had been told to take Class A 0–6–0 No.3637 light engine to Sleaford for the purpose of working a freight from there to Colwick Yard near Nottingham. George drew his oil allowance from the stores and whilst he oiled the side rods, axleboxes and motion-work of the cylinders, I made up the fire, checked the injectors and cracked some of the bigger lumps of coal. Then I fitted, one back and one front, the two headlamps that I had drawn from the oil stores. The standard time allowance for the preparation of No.3637, as a medium-sized engine, was forty-five minutes. Well within that time we were standing at the shed outlet with George phoning the signalman to let us out for Sleaford. Off we went with well-cleaned No.3637, her brisk exhaust beats and the powerful-sounding thumps of her side rods giving a really business-like impression.

Our train was waiting for us in a siding at Sleaford. The guard came up, telling George that we should run under Class A timings directly to Colwick Yard; fairly sharp timings for ordinary freight work. The guard then took George's daily ticket or timesheet away with him, for the former always entered the passing times, loads conveyed, as well as any lost time, on the driver's ticket. The headlamps were now re-arranged on the smokebox top and over the lefthand buffer in order to make plain to each signalman that a Class A train was passing his box.

No.3637 started off bravely for Colwick but, to me as a novice, the pulling seemed hard. Looking back, I could see that immediately behind the engine there were more than a dozen wagons loaded with lumber, obviously from Boston docks, whilst goodness only knows what was in the wagons further back. There had been plenty of water and steam in the boiler when we started, as well as a good fire, yet very soon the steam pressure was slowly but surely falling back.

After passing Rauceby station, I looked up from my firing and peered ahead through the round spectacle glass.

The chimney exhaust was lifting up rapid spurts of blackish smoke straight up into the air whilst the smokebox swayed gently in rhythm with the strokes of the two pistons in the cylinders below it. On the footplate one could clearly feel the intense strain as the engine exerted full power. We had already begun to climb in earnest the limestone hump that lies across the floor of that geological feature known as the Ancaster Gap in the long and almost unbroken Lincolnshire Edge.

Wilsford box signals were at clear and the gradient increased. George pushed the reversing lever farther forward, to let more steam into the cylinders. I intended to try and hold the steam pressure by not putting any more cold water into the boiler, but George called over "Better put your injector on!" My side of the job was going from bad to worse and even if it was only my second run I felt pretty awful about it. In spite of my best efforts to place coal evenly over the firebed, as well as the fact that the fire appeared to be burning all right, the pressure was now down to under 140. George looked anxious, yet did not interfere with what I was doing. He kept the regulator wide open, forcing the 0–6–0 to push her way along with what steam she had got. Beyond Wilsford level crossing, the line curved right slightly as it entered a cutting, deep within cream-coloured limestone walls. We were now coming to the steepest part of the bank, where the line clung to the northern rim of this eastward-sloping valley.

For the next three miles every exhaust beat was hard and ponderous as our engine struggled to lift the heavy train over the crest of Ancaster bank. There were one or two stretches at 1 in 100 to contend with and I was expecting all the time that we should come to a stand. What a relief it was when Ancaster station came into sight, and with it the top of the bank! No.3637 put her head down the slope and George partly closed the regulator as soon as the pace of the train began to quicken. It had been a near thing, we had little more than 120lb of steam, with the boiler water almost

G.C. 'Tiny' or R.O.D. No.394 (L.N.E.R. No.5394); the O.4 class was widely used for army work overseas during the 1914–1918 war.
[Author's Collection]

Class K2 'Ragtime' No.4635 on a stopping train at Welwyn. This was an early Gresley design for the G.N.R.
[Author's Collection]

out of sight in the gauge glasses. Not a very good second trip for a young fireman!

Soon the wagons began to push us from behind so that very little steam was needed to reach Honington. How much better I felt to be in that happy situation! At Barkston East box we continued westwards under the main line and round the back of Gonerby to the Nottingham line at Allington Junction. George, not knowing whether there would be a queue of trains waiting to get into Colwick Yard, as was often the case, decided to stop for water at Aslockton where a steam-driven pump supplied the overhead water tank. All along this section of the line it is pretty flat country and proved easy-going for No.3637. At Radcliffe-on-Trent we came to the massive steel girder bridge that crossed the River Trent and, very soon afterwards, we branched right into the big freight yard at Colwick.

★ ★ ★

The General Strike intervened at this time in May 1926. It began on Tuesday the 4th and lasted nine days, Britain's railways never being quite the same again. Whilst freight traffic on the railways was stopped, road transport was able to prove itself as a cheap door-to-door form of transportation, and never looked back.

I was out until early in June when I was called back, not for cleaning engines, but to work on loading locomotive coal from a small reserve stack of a few hundred tons in the engine shed yard at Sleaford. As the miners were still on strike, no colliery coal was available, so the railway had to turn to its stockpiles. There were about a dozen cleaners on the job at Sleaford, shovelling coal off the ground into wagons.

The following week we were transferred to the Loco Yard at Grantham where there were some enormous coal stacks, eight to ten feet high and twenty yards wide, each containing thousands of tons of coal. Sleaford had been merely a warming-up exercise for the Grantham job, which called for a gang of at least twenty cleaners.

Alongside each coal stack was a length of track on which stood empty wagons. Now, it was easy throwing the lumps off the near and top edge into the wagons below, but once that had been done the work became progressively more difficult. Coal had to be carried further, big pieces in our hands and the smaller stuff on shovels, whilst from the middle of the stack wheelbarrows were used. We were supervised by an old ashfiller, who estimated and recorded each cleaner's results, for we were on piecework. For the first and easiest part of the stack we received 1½d a ton, 2½d for the middle section, and 3½d for the outside – the latter being the part farthest away. On top of this we did have a basic wage, but it was necessary to work very hard if one wished to earn anything worthwhile. In order to provide some work for as many cleaners as possible, it was a three-day week for everybody, and we all signed on as unemployed for the other three days. Actually, however, our railway and Labour Exchange money combined left us better off than if we had been cleaning engines full time.

By the time that all ground stocks had been picked up, locomotive coal began to arrive from Poland, Germany, Belgium and the U.S.A. Eventually, about August, all the cleaners were back on full time cleaning, but it was a lot longer before I got any more firing work.

★ ★ ★

Mention has already been made how, during the 1925 locomotive exchanges, the G.W. Castles beat the Pacifics. Even prior to this some of Gresley's personal assistants had tried to persuade him to alter the valve gear settings, without success. When the results of the trials were known, it strengthened the arguments of these assistants to the extent that, grudgingly, Gresley agreed to experiment. Pacific No.4477 *Gay Crusader* of Doncaster Carr shed would be given valve heads that had 3/8" additional lap in order to see what difference it made. Late in the summer of 1926 this locomotive began her trials on Doncaster – King's Cross – Doncaster trains. Word soon got round among the Grantham enginemen and staff that 4477 was running experimentally with GW type piston valve heads, and that she was doing quite well.

It so happened that another passed cleaner and I were sent one afternoon to meet *Gay Crusader* with the northbound train in the station in order to throw coal forward from the back of her tender during the three minutes booked stop. There was nothing unusual in this, because 'getting coal forward, was a job that was often done as a help to firemen on long runs like this – 156 miles from King's Cross to Doncaster. The train came in; we jumped up into the cab promptly, threw our shovels over the tender top, climbed after them and began shovelling coal forward as hard as we could go. Before we had moved half a ton, the Doncaster firemen called out, "That will do!" although he had less coal in the shovelling hole than was usual to take him to Doncaster. As we climbed back over the tender front, it was noticeable that both driver and fireman were happy and relaxed and there was plenty of steam showing on the gauge.

One of Gresley's assistants, a man of about thirty, was riding on the footplate, noting the progress of the long-lap trials. He was standing on the platform talking to the afternoon running foreman who had come over to see the train out, and they were discussing things. I heard the assistant say to the foreman, "When we took her (4477) out for the first time after the valves had been altered, we all knew at once that we had a wonderfully improved engine. As soon as we got to King's Cross, I went straight into Mr. Gresley's office and told him about it." Gresley listened, but remained rather sceptical and all he said was that he would ride with the engine himself tomorrow. It seems that the Chief went and was convinced at long last. Certainly the alteration was a great success. *Gay Crusader*, hauling 500-ton trains, now ran fast and free with a shorter cut-off, burnt less coal and was a livelier engine altogether. Further, it was soon decided to add long travel valves and accept the Great Western principles of steam distribution.

Pacific No.2555 *Centenary*, with valves moving an extra $1\frac{3}{16}''$, began her trials early in 1927. Once again the results were remarkable, drivers being able to notch up to 18 per cent cut-off. No.2555 revelled in this treatment, racing up and down the old Great Northern main line as light and free-running as a hare. Instead of the usual Pacific coal consumption of about 50lbs a mile when hauling 500-ton trains, *Centenary* managed on a little less than 40lbs.

Thereafter, as each Pacific passed through the Works for general repairs, newstyle long travel and long lap valves were fitted. Up to then, it had been a tradition on the G.N. for drivers to run at speed with the regulator half open, and the reverser pulled up to give a 40 per cent cut-off. This now had to be altered. A type-written notice was posted in the time office at Grantham telling drivers that, with the altered Pacifics, the best results would be obtained from a fully open regulator and a cut-off of around 25 per cent when running at speed. The time had come for the regulator to be left in the open position; any variation of the effort of the engine should be controlled by the reversing screw.

To the lineside observer, instead of the former hard exhausts heard at the chimney tops, there were now softer chuffs as the Pacifics played with their work.

Late in 1927 there appeared the super-Pacifics with larger superheaters and boiler steam pressure increased from 180lb. to 220lb. These super-Pacifics burned only 36lb. to the mile, at once laying open the way to non-stop running between London and Edinburgh. On 1st May 1928 No.4472 *Flying Scotsman* made the first non-stop run of 397 miles between the two capitals. Later on came the stream-lined A.4 class, of which No.4468 *Mallard* is perhaps best known, as holder of the steam speed record. On 3rd July 1938, whilst working (ostensibly) a special train for some braking trials be-

Smoke and steam at King's Cross in the 1920s; Atlantic No. 4436 leaves with a Pullman.
[Author's Collection]

tween Barkston and Peterborough, a speed of 126 miles an hour was recorded on the falling gradient of 1 in 240 between Little Bytham and Essendine. Gresley was in the train, driver Duddington of Doncaster was on *Mallard*, and riding with him was locomotive inspector Sam Jenkins. Sam often talked about that run in later years; how the driver asked whether he should, at the crucial moment, give the engine a bit more cut-off, and how on arrival at Peterborough, the middle big end was found all broken up by the great strain placed upon it.

CHAPTER SIX

More Firing Turns

AT 7.0AM ONE October morning in 1926, I signed on with passed fireman Fred Crowson, who had been told to relieve a set of Doncaster men and work their coal train to Peterborough. This train stood on the slow line alongside the up goods yard with ex-Great Central 2–8–0 No.5382 at the head of it. This type of engine was variously known as a 'Tiny' or an 'R.O.D.' – tiny because they were so big and R.O.D. because the Royal Ordnance Department had chosen them for war work abroad during the 1914–1918 War.

When we climbed into the cab, the driver reported to Fred, "All right – nothing wrong with her." With that, he and his mate picked up their food boxes, and with a "Cheerio" they were gone. It was my first time on an R.O.D. as well as my first trip to Peterborough. Still, I had heard the senior passed cleaners speak well of these 2–8–0s but, all the same, I felt rather nervous, remembering the 'down on steam' run with No.3637 over Ancaster bank. The main line route in front of us, I reflected, started with a long climb up to Stoke Tunnel.

The signal was lowered, Fred gave a short blast on the deep-toned G.C. whistle, wound the screw reverser out into the forward position and, taking the sloping one-sided regulator handle in both hands, pulled it upwards towards him. No. 5382 responded sturdily with the first of a series of long deep 'whoofs' and moved off in a determined way. Fred called over to me to ask, "Been on one of these before?" I shook my head. "Keep up a good fire and plenty of water in the boiler, and you'll be all right," he replied with a grin. We passed high over the River Witham at Saltersford, climbing up the 1 in 198 very nicely, with the up and down main lines on our right.

My first fears began to subside when I saw that No. 5382 held a full head of steam – it was certainly easy work firing to an R.O.D. Six or seven shovelfuls of coal thrown through the round firehole door at short intervals seemed all that was needed to ensure that we had a full head of steam. Deep down in the limestone cutting, that big old G.C. engine thumped her way up to Great Ponton station. The ponderous regular exhaust beats spoke back to us with absolute assurance. DAMN – AND – BUGG – ER – PE – TER – BO – RO was one way to put into words the way those fine old freighters expressed themselves as they climbed up to Stoke on that five-mile grade. J. G. Robinson, when he built his 2–8–0s, had put plenty of metal into them – 120 tons of it – for there were none of the wriggles one endured on a G.N. engine.

At High Dyke signalbox, on the north side of Stoke Tunnel, we had to wait a path through the two-line tunnel that bores its way, in blue clay, for 880 yards through Bassingthorpe Hill, still climbing up the gradient.

In order to avoid firing inside the tunnel, I built up the fire as we moved up towards it. This led to a lot of thick smoke, so much so, in fact, that when No. 5382 thrust into the tunnel mouth she was engulfed in a frightful pother of thick black smoke. About half-way through the tunnel, the driving wheels started to slip like mad, with the engine dancing up and down in a useless manner. Doubtless we had hit a place where water dripping from the roof had made the rails wet and greasy. Fred shut and re-opened the regulator, but every time that steam went back into the engine's two cylinders, the wheels spun again. Speed fell quickly, whilst my extra smoke filled the cab down to our waists – and really thick choking G.C. smoke it was, too. "We are going to stick," shouted Fred. "If she stops, you get down on your side – I will stop on her." Then, just as I was thinking of getting down my side, and wondering whether it would be any better standing on the footsteps between engine and tunnel wall, No. 5382 stopped slipping. She again put down her feet in firm fashion, soon picked up speed and went steadily forward as if nothing had happened. We passed out of the tunnel into daylight with our 500 tons of coal handled in fine style, continued up to Stoke signalbox, and surmounted the crest of the bank at the hundredth mile post. The climb was now over. All that No. 5382 had to do was hold the unbraked train back down the long run down of nearly twenty miles into Peterborough. Fred and I could enjoy the ride.

As we ran down the first ten miles of that rolling south Lincolnshire countryside, I looked out over the autumn landscape of lineside fields. Here and there stood an isolated farmhouse surrounded by newly-built corn stacks, whilst in places there were villages or small groups of houses. In odd corners, often behind tall elm trees, stood an occasional limestone-walled parish church. Meanwhile the line sliced through humps of land in cuttings, or spanned the hollows on embankments. Fast expresses overhauled us on our right, or slammed past at great speed in the opposite direction.

The number of signals increased as we came closer to Peterborough. At the Rhubarb Bridge we went under the Midland & Great Northern line before being turned to the left round the back of New England loco depot. We ran beside the long rows of railway houses known as the Barracks, of uniform dreariness, and crept forward into Spital Goods Yard, the destination of our load of coal. We then took our engine light into New England depot where the Running Foreman told us to leave it on the ashpit and go home passenger. All in all, my first trip to Peterborough had been most enjoyable.

By way of a change, just before Christmas I found myself with another passed fireman, Dick Widdowson, working a pick-up goods to Leicester. Dick was a portly roundish man, considered by many to be on the miserable side, but I found that underneath he liked a joke and was a pleasant enough mate on the footplate. We relieved a Newark crew on No.4143 at Harby and Stathern station, which is in the Vale of Belvoir and the fox-hunting country around Belvoir Castle. I well remember how clean and tidy the inside of the cab was when we took over the little 0–6–0 Class B. It was a wintry day outside under a grey sky that promised snow any moment, but the fire in the firebox burned bright and warm, whilst all the brass fittings shone with the glitter of Christmas, and we were very cosy indeed.

We soon set off with our short train of about twenty wagons, and had gone only a few miles before Dick called out to me, "Ever seen a real steam engine, mate?" He jerked his head backwards, beckoning me over to his side. Approaching us was an L.M.S. Willesden – Colwick freight. The chimney, smokebox front and the red buffer beam of the engine pulling it could be seen, but the rest of it was hidden by clouds of steam leaking from the piston and valve rod glands. "You can always tell an old North Western one – you can never see them for steam," said Dick with a grin as he enjoyed what he most likely thought was his Christmas joke. How the L.M.S. crew ever saw their signals through that moving screen of steam, I do not know. In contrast, our little engine was beautifully tight all across her front end. As the L.M.S. engine slowly overhauled us, I saw that it was an ex-L.N.W.R. 0–8–0 of the 'D' type that had no flanges on the third pair of wheels.

Between Melton Mowbray and Lowesby it began to snow heavily – what a perfect Christmas setting all this was! Big flakes came spinning crazily round the chimney or dome to hit against the cab front and swirl past us madly in all directions. We left our train in the goods yard at Leicester Belgrave Road station and went home light engine to Grantham, amid a landscape white and silent.

Earlier on in these pages, I mentioned how the little 0–6–0 engines often used to get stuck in their attempts to pull freights out of the lay-by siding at Barkston. This was still a regular occurrence and during one evening in January 1927 we went with 4–4–0 No.4327 to help a train out. We went tender-first to Barkston, crossed over, backed carefully on to the front of the old Class B, and soon both engines were stepping it out nicely up the Grantham. Although our engine had 6′8″ wheels for passenger work, our extra power tipped the balance all right. If only the old G.N. had built some 2–8–0 engines of the G.C. 'Tiny' class and put them on the Doncaster to Peterborough, or Retford to Peterborough, coal trains, what a lot of trouble would have been saved!

In order to avoid any further trouble, it was decided that we should double-head this particular train over the top of the bank at Stoke. As we plodded up the grade, it was rather interesting to listen to the exhaust beats of the two engines, for the faster beats of the smaller-wheeled engine behind our tender contrasted with the much slower count of our 'W' class 4–4–0.

At Corby we came off and returned home tender-first just after midnight. A bitterly keen north-east wind was blowing, which did its best to freeze our blood. Running tender-first in the depth of winter was always a shockingly cold experience.

Whilst we were disposing No.4327 on the ashpit, one of the big superheated Ivatt-designed 4–4–0s came up behind us. My driver, Ted Wright, who was one of the biggest and tallest of the Grantham enginemen, looked at it and then told me how one of its class, probably No.3060 or 3061, worked the special two-coach train that took Lord Kitchener in June 1916 to Scotland en route for Scapa Flow on his proposed military mission to Russia. That, of course, was

Kitchener's last journey because the cruiser H.M.S. *Hampshire* was sunk by a German mine shortly after leaving Scapa Flow. According to Ted, those large superheated 4–4–0s were fast runners but terribly bad steamers.

The conversation turned from Kitchener to the post-Armistice times of 1918–1919. Ted had been with an army railway unit moving stores back from the British lines on the Western Front. He told me how whole train-loads of stores used to be stopped at wayside stations, where the disposable stuff was sold to any French people who cared to come and buy. I gathered that Ted had, by this dishonesty made quite a bit of money to bring home.

The following February I had my first trip on an ex-Great Eastern engine, and a jolly good run it was, too. Mat Hudson was my driver. Our orders were to go passenger to Sleaford to relieve March depot men on a train of coal empties, and work these forward to Colwick. When the train came in, with 0–6–0 No.8224 at the head, we found the March crew were rather put out about being relieved. They claimed they were booked to lodge at Langwith and had all their food packed up with them so didn't want to get off the engine. However, in the end, they left the cab, althought without saying a word to us about the state of the engine, something that seldom happened when crews changed over.

It was quite a change standing in the comfortable and side-windowed cab of No.8224, for no G.N. freight engine had a roomy cab like this. This engine, built at Stratford Works before the 1914 War, had a broad-topped Belpaire firebox, weighed 76 tons and her power rating was slightly greater than that of G.N. No.3637 of my previous run out of Sleaford. Mat walked round the engine, touching each wheel hub with the back of his hand to make sure that he hadn't taken over any hot bearing. On my side, there was plenty of steam and water in the boiler, but we certainly had a rum-looking lot of coal in the tender. It was foreign stuff, probably Polish – mostly black dust with scarcely a lump to be seen in it. When I lowered the large firehole door flat on to the footboards, the fire inside resembled what I had always imagined the crater of a volcano looked like at close quarters. There was a grey crust over the top of the firebed, punctured with several crater-like holes through which a few bright flames curled up from a cherry-red fire below. My immediate reaction was that I was in for another, and probably worse, trip than before. Yet I knew that the G.E. fireman had brought the engine in in good form.

As soon as we started off with our forty or so coal wagons bound for the Nottinghamshire collieries, I began to fire up. To my amazement, each shovelful, as it fell on to the fire, instantly burst into a blazing fury of intensely hot flame. The pressure held and the 0–6–0 pulled with considerable effort. Among G.N. men there was widespread opinion that the Great Eastern, with its rural lines among the fields of East Anglia, wasn't much of a show, but I began to realise they built some good freight engines at Stratford, if No.8224 was anything to go by.

Between Rauceby and Wilsford Level Crossing signalbox a funny thing happened. We had reached the climb up to Ancaster, but Mat could not push the two-handed regulator handle over into the fully open position in order to give the engine full steam for the extra effort needed. Push or pull as he might, the handle would not go over; it was as if the regulator valve in the dome had come up against a metal stop, and No.8224 was definitely slowing up. "I can't get into second regulator at all," he called out, with a puzzled look on his face, "she's stopping!" Now, it had been my luck to read a magazine article about G.E. engines, in which it had been mentioned how sometimes the pressure of steam bearing on the flat regulator valves held them so fast on their faces that the regulator could not be moved over. "Put her in mid gear, then it will go," I suggested. As he had no alternative, Mat wound the reverser wheel up into mid-gear position – and over the regulator handle went at little more than finger pressure. As smartly as he had wound up, Mat wound out again into full fore gear. No.8224 responded with a series of really loud 'whoofs' as she put her entire power into hauling the train hooked at the rear of her tender. She took the rest of that bank in her stride, with a full head of steam and a boiler full of water. The trick had been getting into mid-gear and stopping the flow of steam into the cylinders whereby the regulator valve was made to float with an equal pressure on both sides of it . . .

At Allington Junction we were held up by signals for ten minutes or so. Knowing the fire had a lot of clinker in it, I started to throw some of it out, although Mat said to me, "Let it stay!" But a dirty fire always hurt me as much as it did the engine, so I fished out, through the firehole, several whacking lumps all red-hot, and pitched them down the bank. I felt a little better after seeing that lot of dross go out, but I knew that there was still almost a foot of clinker all over the firebars. Yet for the rest of the run to Colwick, in spite of the clinker, that old G.E. locomotive steamed well.

The eight mile-long High Dyke to Stainby and Sproxton single line branch was a very busy piece of line, carrying mostly iron ore. Laid down shortly after the 1914–1918 War, it tapped the iron ore reserves of south-west Lincolnshire. I had one trip only over this line when I fired to passed fireman 'Trooper' Henson on 0–6–0 No.3040, starting from Grantham with a train of empty ore wagons plus one or two loaded wagons of coal.

High Dyke is the local name for the Ermine Street of Roman times that passes under the main line about half a mile north of Stoke Tunnel. Between the box and the tunnel there were several sidings for the storage of loaded trains, but it was necessary to back up a special ramp north of the box in order to gather speed for the ascent of the first incline on to the single line. Train working was controlled by an electric token, carried in a leather pouch, and applying to Skillington Junction.

No sooner had I collected my token from the High Dyke signalman than Trooper opened out and away we went down the ramp to take the climb on to the branch in a businesslike manner. Once over the first hill-top we had to keep a sharp look-out, for there were several unstaffed level crossings where cart tracks or country lanes passed over the metals. It was a lovely day of early spring, white fleecy clouds blowing across the sky. Farmers with their horse teams were seeding barley and everything seemed right with the world. The south-east wind, too, played pranks with our puffs of smoke, at first bearing them down from the engine's chimney, then sent them scudding or rolling at low height over the brown earth of the fields.

We had to have one fault, of course, and that was that No.3040's vacuum brake did not hold too well. This did not suit Trooper, a very timid driver at any time, for he insisted that I kept the tender hand brake screwed down hard whenever we dropped down any gradient. And that line was all ups and downs, for the minimum amount of money had been spent on cuttings or embankments when it was built.

At Colsterworth, we stopped to set down our wagons of coal in the station sidings. From there we went on with the empty ore wagons towards Skillington Junction, up-hill and down-dale running all the time. In the bottom of a deepish hollow there was Green Lane level crossing, with its white gates displaying their usual red disc emblem, closed across the railway. We had to stop here and it was my duty to open the gates for our train. Trooper started down very carefully indeed with No.3040. He kept the handle of the vacuum brake down most of the time and told me to see if I could get the hand brake on a little harder. That old engine grunted and knocked, the brake blocks squealed and every time Trooper eased the vacuum a fraction, she certainly lurched forward. Down went the vacuum brake handle on to its stop but with so little effect that Trooper snatched the reversing lever back into full backwards gear. With much shaking and bucking, we slowed, and crept down to the gates, before thankfully coming to a stand in the right place.

When I climbed back into the cab after opening the gates, Trooper said to me nervously, "I'll book this brake when we get back!" He was quite shaken.

At Skillington Junction our electric token was surrendered to the signalman, who then gave us a train staff that authorised us to go on to the Sproxton iron-ore quarries. Here large mechanical shovels scooped up the reddish-brown material known as Northampton Sand Ore. How many millions of tons of it have been scraped off the earth's surface there I do not know, but it is certainly a huge figure. In 1927 there were five trains a day and ten years later the traffic had risen to fifteen trains a day. But the ore had a relatively low content of iron, leading eventually to preference for higher-grade foreign ores and the closing of the line in the 1960s.

If ever I meet Trooper Henson in heaven, I am quite sure that the first thing I shall say to him is, "Do you remember that day we had with No.3040 on the High Dyke?" In spite of the brake trouble however, I thoroughly enjoyed my day on that really rural freight line.

The 2–6–0 K2Mogul, or Ragtime, as the men called the class, was Gresley's first contribution to the Great Northern locomotive stock. They always impressed me very much and, although when they got on to other sections of the L.N.E.R., they were cursed right and left, I liked them. I remember one hot July afternaan in 1927 I went with Tommy Ross, a perky, thick-set driver who always wore his uniform cap at a jaunty angle, on Ragtime No.4655 hauling empty passenger stock to Doncaster. She rode a bit rough, but steamed well and thumped her way along beautifully. As we ran down through Newark and Retford, what a pleasure it was to lean out on my side and listen to the lovely sound PLINKA – PLONKA coming from her rotating motion. These engines won their nickname because ragtime music was the craze at the time of their building and engine crews were quick to make the comparison with the engine sounds. A month firing nothing but Ragtimes would have been fine for me, but in fact I never fired another.

When platelayer Jack Stead came home at noon from Barkston station one Saturday soon after this he brought me a phoned message from the loco that I was to report for duty at 10.0pm. Foreman Bill Richardson was on the night shift and as soon as he saw me said there was a firing turn for me double-heading on the 1.8am to York (10.35pm King's Cross to Edinburgh). This was with passed fireman Mat Hudson who would book on just before midnight and meanwhile I was to assist on the ashpit. A marvellous piece of luck!

When Mat signed on, I joined him and together we prepared No.4399, a Class W 4–4–0 from Colwick which had a nice clean appearance. This extra engine was needed because an additional two coaches were to be put on the back of the train at Grantham, bringing the load over the 350-ton Atlantic limit. Mat told me that the night express would come in with a Peterborough engine and crew, and that we were going tandem as the second engine. The rule was that the driver booked to work the train always went in front, where he had the best view of all the signals and, incidentally, had prior control over the brake. Yet Mat would be equally responsible for the observance of all signals and for the general safety of the train.

Promptly at 1.5am the express came in with Atlantic No.3281 at the front. As she rolled gently to a stand, her polished boiler and tender sides reflected the light of the platform lamps. A shunter quickly uncoupled her from the first coach, the Peterborough driver ran ahead towards the North signalbox, and we were called out from the short engine-waiting dock on to the main line before setting back on to the train. Back came the Atlantic for her coupling up. The shunter climbed up on to the platform, calling out to both drivers, "Blow up!" so that they might test the vacuum brakes. There were two needles on an engine vacuum gauge, one on either side, indicating separately the vacuum in the train pipe and on the top sides of the pistons in the engine brake cylinders. Mat and I scanned our gauge as the needles crept steadily up to twenty-one inches of vacuum, the correct reading.

Both engines, with steam blowing off noisily at their safety valves, stood like iron race horses raring to go. The Peterborough driver stepped down on to the platform, where he and Mat exchanged a few words together before they both came back to their engines. They had agreed that we should pick up water first at the track troughs, as was the usual practice. If the leading engine dipped its scoop first and the fireman was slow getting it out, or it stuck down, all the water would be thrown out of the trough and we should get none.

Porters' whistles sounded along the platform – it was time to start! Looking back I saw the light in the platform inspector's lamp turned to green. "Right away!" I called out to Mat. He leaned forward over his reversing screw to peer through the round spectacle glass for a final check that the signal was still showing green. As he stood there with his left hand ready on the regulator, the flashing light of the fire lit up the left side of his calm face. Mat popped his whistle, our Peterborough friend popped his in acknowledgement. Mat tugged at the regulator – followed by a sensation of a slight movement under our feet. The Atlantic in front sent up her first puff of smoke and steam – then slipped madly for a moment, with a great column of steam and smoke, lit by the station lamps, ascending straight up into the night sky. We were off on our 83-mile non-stop run to York . . .

Keeping the regulator almost wide open, with the reverser screw well down in fore gear, Mat made No. 4399 do her full share at getting up speed. As we gradually got into a canter he eased up on the regulator and pulled up the reverser until the engine sounded and felt less pushed. By the time that we thundered through Barkston, with a bump and a clatter from the points, our speed of around sixty had ironed out the individual knocks and noises into a blend of fast rat – a – tat – tats.

Steaming well, No.4399 maintained boiler pressure quite nicely. The fast chimney exhaust whipped the fire into a frenzy of white flame which had such an eager appetite for oxygen that a fan-like sheet of flame licked constantly along the outer edge of the firehole. Immediately I finished each round of firing, I took the hammer and cracked up several big lumps of coal into pieces about the size of a half pound of butter, in readiness for the next round.

As far as Barkston I had known the signals, but after that I was lost. Whenever I looked out on my side of the cab, ahead of our engine was the swaying dark shape of the Atlantic leading us. She was rolling about in a lively manner, swaying from side to side in unison with our engine coupled behind her. From the Atlantic's cab window on my side a beam of firelight ran along the side of a cutting like the bright blade of a knife. And what a sharp short flash there was when that ray of light hit the abutment of a bridge over the tracks! Light from the Atlantic's firehole also lit up the underside of her smoke as it trailed backwards, another spectacular night-time scene with darker colours in it. Both engines made a lot of noise, with the ring of steel from their motion blending with the fast exhaust beats of their chimneys. My chief concern, however, was the fire. As soon as it looked really white, a sign that it was getting burnt down, I banged in another five or six shovelfuls, carefully spreading them over the whole of the firegrate. Fast-running engines tended to work the coal on the firebars towards the front end under the brick arch, so rather more coal was spread under the firehole door at the near end.

We speeded relentlessly onwards through Hougham and Claypole, country stations that to me were mere shadows and bumps in the night. Newark was hit with a smack. Quick to follow was the boom of the overhead girderwork on the River Trent Bridge. Beyond it lay Muskham water troughs with Trent water in them. Mat knew exactly where to dip and, although it was really my job to work the scoop, he did it for me. The instant he pulled out the long handle on the tender front my side, we heard water rushing up into the tender. At the same time there was a sensation of a slight steadying up of our speed due to the drag of the scoop in the water. Ours was down only for a few seconds and, as it was lifted, splashes from the Atlantic in front told us that they now were getting water.

Carlton and Crow Park stations flashed by. Soon we came to the three miles climb at 1 in 200 up Weston bank, approached on a long left-hand curve. Mat came over to my side for a sight of the Weston distant. "Whenever you come down here, kid," he shouted above the din, "you have to look across the fields for the Weston distant. Can you see it over there?" A short shower of rain crossed our path, littering drops that hit my peering face like hail stones. At Retford, where the old Great Central line to Immingham crossed our main line at right angles, No.4399 shook herself sharply as our wheels met the track gaps below.

It was not a particularly dark night, but as we pounded along through those parts of Lincolnshire then, Nottinghamshire and Yorkshire, there were very few lights to be seen. Fewer cars used the roads at night in those days, nor were the towns lit up with the garish street lighting we know at present. It was in the Doncaster area, with its big goods yards, street lights and the outside lighting on colliery sidings near the line that we met the first glitter of lamplight.

At twenty minutes to three we ran slowly down the long curving platform at York station. Both engines, still coupled together, ran off the train to go into York loco. When I looked at the fire, I saw at once that I had brought in a needlessly big accumulation of half-burnt coal. This was my own fault, because shortly before we reached Selby, Mat had advised me not to put any more coal on; but I suppose I thought that I knew best. The fireman who was given the job of throwing out that fire must have said more than a few uncomplimentary things about me!

Mat came back from the foreman with instructions to leave No.4399, eat our meal in the foreign enginemen's messroom, and then take charge of a Peterborough Atlantic (No.3281) in readiness to work a special passenger-rated parcels train. York shed had prepared this Atlantic for us to take back, so all we had to do after eating was to climb aboard all ready to go. Dawn had just broken over a cloud-ribbed sky as we backed out of the loco, switched over the main line north of the station with our tender wheels squealing at the sharp curves and eventually came to a stand in a short siding to await being called forward through the station. Half a mile to the east, silhouettcd against the brightening sky, stood the grey-towered pile of York Minster.

About 5.0am the signal came off, calling us through the station to back on to the parcels train which was ready to depart. The moment that we set off south, how marked was the difference between wheezy No.4399 and purposeful No3281! The lively way in which the latter pulled away was noticeable straightaway. Mat too, as he stood on his driver's footstool behind the reversing lever, looked very pleased with himself. He pressed the 4–4–2 along in a businesslike manner that was exhilarating. But only half a mile or so out of York steam pressure began falling back. We both looked at the gauge. "What's wrong?" said Mat as if, like me, he did not know why anything should be amiss. Checking, I saw that the ashpan damper door had not been opened, an omission that was smartly remedied, and round came the needle on the steam gauge. By the time that Mat shut off steam for the 45m.p.h. restriction over the swing bridge at Selby over the river Ouse, we had so much steam that it was blowing off madly at the safety valves.

Our first stop was at Doncaster where, as we ran slowly beside the up platform, night-weary porters lolled against loaded parcels trolleys. The station foreman came up to us, telling Mat that the train would be ready in about five minutes, first stop Peterborough. When he had gone, Mat turned to me and said that he was not going past Grantham. He had booked on duty twice the previous day, was tired, and Grantham was his limit.

We left at 6.00am on our 50½-mile run to Grantham with Mat driving as if he were riding the favourite in the St. Leger. The Atlantic took up the challenge, for she fairly raced along with the light train of only six bogie parcels vans. Every time that I slid half a dozen shovelfuls of coal through the firehole, the whole firebox was set ablaze with a mass of dazzling incandescent flame. The faster we went, the more steam we seemed to have in hand, the needle holding between 170 and 175lb all the time. Getting more water into the boiler was no problem either, for the exhaust injector on my side worked splendidly and did not knock the steam pressure back very much each time that it was applied.

The gradient up to Askham Tunnel took a slight toll on our home-bound gallop, but after we had slipped over the top, there was no holding the 4–4–2 back. It was Sunday morning, when few trains were about, so we had a clear path, with every signal arm hanging down obligingly to beckon us on. No sooner had signalboxes or cottages beside level crossings appeared ahead, than we had reached and passed them with a wham.

We recrossed the Trent in a resounding rumble, thundered on through Newark to pass Claypole and Hougham with No.3281 giving the impression that she was a thunderbolt on iron wheels. It is true that our speed was checked slightly again after Hougham as we climbed up that open countryside of clayland humps, yet we still went at a great rate. Shortly after bursting out of Peasecliff Tunnel, the 280′ high steeple of Grantham parish church became visible on the left of the line. At fourteen minutes to seven o'clock, No.3281 came clanking to a stand under the home signal at the south end of the up platform, in spite of the fact that it was at clear for us to run past it and on to Peterborough.

Mat Hudson, looking a little smug, wiped his hands

slowly and unnecessarily on a sponge cloth. He then told me to run over to the loco for a relief crew to take the train forward. "There's a good ten minutes or so to spare," he said as I got down from the engine. Running Foreman Fred Button was talking to the Sunday morning shed shunt crew outside the time office when I arrived. "Get your food boxes and off you go to Peterborough," he instructed them after I had passed my message.

Mat, of course, had brought the train in ten minutes early in order to ensure that, without causing any delay, he did not have to go through to Peterborough. In retrospect, this was probably the best of all my footplate runs, completely confirming all that I had ever heard about the wonders of the fast-running and free-steaming G.N. superheated Atlantics.

CHAPTER SEVEN

Goodbye to Grantham

GRANTHAM IN THE late 1920s was a good depot for any young fireman. It was not too large, whilst the number of express passenger turns allocated to the shed provided splendid opportunities for ocassional fast work. Grantham station was also quite a busy location on the LNER. Some idea of the traffic may be gained from the following list of booked movements in the up direction (southbound) each weekday:

Express passenger	21
Stopping passenger	5
Express freight	20
Ordinary freight	10
Coal trains (some 10 000 tons of coal)	26
Empty iron ore trains	2
Branch line passenger (terminating)	24
Branch line freight	5
Total =	113

The pattern of the down trains was very similar except, of course, that the coal traffic was represented by empty wagons returning to the Derbyshire, Nottinghamshire and South Yorkshire collieries. A fair estimate is that an average of ten trains an hour either used the station or passed through it each weekday – an average of one every six minutes.

However, for me, a youthful urge of mild wanderlust had built up in my blood. I wanted to see a little more of the world and the best way to begin seemed to be a move south on the LNER. At that time it was the practice to advertise vacancies for passed cleaners within defined promotional areas. I applied successfully to go to Hatfield.

My years at Grantham had been happily and usefully spent. I had made friendships that have lasted a lifetime, not to mention the wealth of experience I had gained in my introduction to the railway at that famous Lincolnshire depot of the old LNER. On 3rd September 1927, with 101 firing turns to my credit, I travelled south to Hatfield.

Hatfield loco, sheltering snugly under some three hundred yards or so of the embankment that formed the western boundary of the line opposite the station, was a relatively small establishment. It was the home of sixteen or so locomotives that worked on the three local branch lines, as well as on the main line suburban passenger service to and from King's Cross. There was nothing out of the ordinary about any of these: two 0–6–0 Humpies for yard shunting, three or four elderly 0–6–0 Class B tender engines for the branch freights, two W Class 4–4–0s, one or two Ivatt 0–6–0 condenser-fitted N1 Class passenger tankies and, at the top of the bill, eight Great Eastern-type 0–6–2 N7 superheated and Westinghouse/vacuum brake fitted comparatively new suburban tank engines.

Twelve or so wooden steps led down from the street into the shed yard. At the bottom of these steps, on the left, was the little hutch-like Running Foremen's office, provided with true Great Northern standards of economy by the simple expedient of sawing off one section or compartment of a condemned coach and setting it down on a sleeper foundation. One of the original coach doors still remained on its hinges. Diogenes in his Grecian tub probably had just about as much room as those Running Foremen: one-legged Jack

Finch, one-eyed Ted Smith and Charlie Torr, who were individually on duty.

The enginemen were better off for accommodation because they had a newish wooden hut, painted cream and brown, for their messroom. Unlike the Grantham men, who seldom bothered to wash before going off duty, these Hertfordshire men reflected their southern refinement by

Grantham Old Shed in B.R. days; 'Ragtime' No.61756 on left, Class 'A' 0–6–0 No.64178 centre and (just visible) Pacific No.60521.
[T.G. Hepburn]

using the messroom basin for a thorough wash with soap and hot water at the end of each day's work. There were no dirty-faced or untidy looking locomotivemen walking about the streets of Hatfield.

A little further north stood an old and largish red brick building, divided into two rooms. The oil and general stores occupied the southern half, whilst the other side was the fitters and boilersmiths' workshop-cum-messroom.

Bob Lawrence, a former Doncaster Plant fitter, now middle-aged, slightly lame, pale and balding, was the leading fitter. He and his red-haired mate Tuppn'y Wren, worked on days only, undertaking the more important jobs, such as big end attention plus periodical examination of valves and pistons. Lawrence was also the man who took out the hand-operated breakdown crane and its toolvan to deal with local minor derailments. Two other fitters, Jack Marsh, a pleasant but dogmatic chap, and George Benyon, an inoffensive Welshman with a pleasing Celtic lilt in his voice, worked on shifts. There was a third, semi-skilled mechanic named Fred Andrews graded as a steam joint maker, who earned but a few shillings more weekly than a plain fitter's mate. Of the two boilersmiths, Harry Mileham, the senior man, was already ageing, as his white wiry moustache and silver hair plainly indicated. Tom Clark, the younger man, had served his boilermaker's apprenticeship in the Clyde shipyards around Glasgow. The awful living conditions up there had made Tom into a red hot Labour man of an amiable but very argumentative type whenever politics became the subject of conversation. No matter what the weather, or the occasion, indoors or out, Tom always wore an open-neck white shirt with a tuft of bushy chest hair showing boldly at the vee of his collar.

Northwards stood the cleaners' messroom, the coal stack, ashpit, water crane, ground level coaling stage and at the end, the engine turntable. The coal stage was another labour intensive affair, more so even than Grantham because the coal tubs had to be hoisted over the engine tenders or bunkers by means of a hand-operated crane. Two coalmen worked on each shift. At loading-up times, they could be seen winding away on either side at handles set at 180 degrees, so that as one man's head went down the other's came up. At each seventeenth turn, as the winding chain began its return run on the roller, the mechanism sent a disconcerting kick through the handles. Coalman Harry Crane had intensely blue eyes and in his younger days had served as a stoker in the Merchant Navy. He told me that whilst crossing the south Pacific at night, he went into the boiler room as a coloured stoker had knifed another coloured stoker and was in the act of pushing the dead body into the boiler furnace. The murderer brandished his knife at Harry, threatening him with the same fate if ever he breathed a word. The captain's enquiry next day failed completely in solving the man's disappearance – all that could be assumed was that he had fallen overboard in the dark.

On the other side of the entrance steps, already mentioned, stood the furnace where sand was dried before it went into the engines sand boxes for use in countering wheel slip on wet rails. Next came the shed itself, with its two roads holding about five engines. Built into the south-east corner of this building was the office of the depot superintendent, who at that time was young and ambitious Bernard Adkinson. His father, known as Black Harry, on account of his black beard, had at one time been a Running Foreman at Grantham. A small wooden hut immediately beyond the shed was the home of the two depot clerks, Charlie Arbour and Len Shepherd.

Firelighting and boilerwashing were done by a pair of men graded as firelighters. They worked two shifts; the day man did the boilerwashing whilst his mate on the night shift undertook all the lighting of engine fires and saw that each engine had a good fire and a small head of steam in readiness for the next day's work. Pottie Wilson, the shorter and older man of the two, had been in Kitchener's Army during World War I in a railway transportation unit on the Western Front in France. In 1915 he had walked seven miles through the narrow lanes from Hatfield to Hertford in order to enlist. Ron Halsey, his mate, had formerly been a booking office clerk, and later a stationary engineman in charge of the steam pump that raised water from a pumphouse south of the station for locomotive use. The three shift-working storesmen combined care of the oil stores with the overlooking of the enginemen's appearance sheets.

On top of the bank stood the lavatory block, simple and plain, as indeed were all such conveniences at Great Northern Section engine sheds. One sat upon a rounded beam of wood over a drain that was flushed violently at intervals from an overhead tank. The cubicles had half doors whilst the toilet paper was, as elsewhere at loco depots, old working timetables or out-of-date fortnightly working notices.

★ ★ ★

Summing up, Hatfield was a family-sized depot where everybody knew everybody else. It was, one may say, ideal for good and efficient working. Bigger locos like New England or King's Cross were more difficult to manage and inevitably had more labour troubles even in those days. Places like Stratford on the G.E. side, with a thousand locomotives, were, in later years, past praying for when it came to counting conduct and performance – or so we thought.

Hatfield town itself was a big improvement on Grantham as a place in which to live. I lodged at 28 Stonecross Road on a newly-built council estate where every house had a pretty garden back and front, and where each window was gay with brightly coloured curtains. This was a pleasant change from the rather drab red brick houses in Cecil Street with their heavily veiled lace-curtained windows relieved occasionally by the display of a rather sad looking aspidistra. From our garden in Stonecross we could look out across the cutting of the St. Albans branch to the great open flint-flecked fields on Dan Crawford's farm. Flowers and fresh air seemed to be the rule everywhere.

One drawback, however, has to be mentioned. In Ground Lane nearby, where the houses were owned by Lord Salisbury, pan closets still persisted. The town council had a horse-drawn night soil cart known as 'The Diamond Cart' that, between ten-thirty and eleven each Tuesday night, came round on its sanitation mission. Passed cleaners like George Tyler, used to the refinements of London, avoided this cart by going the other way round as they returned to their lodgings.

CHAPTER EIGHT

Hertfordshire Branch Lines

EACH OF THE three single-track branch lines worked by Hatfield men and engines meandered through some pretty parts of the Hertfordshire countryside. They are all closed now.

On the Thursday of my first week at Hatfield I had my introduction to this branch work when I fired for elderly driver Ernie Valentine over the ten and a half miles Hatfield to Hertford line. I was lucky enough to get this job, simply because I had gone to Hatfield with a seniority date of 24 March 1924 that put me above quite a number of the other passed cleaners. In fact, it was only on my first day that I did any engine cleaning at all. The chief clerk at Grantham had told me that I was certain to do well for firing turns at Hatfield, and so it turned out to be.

To come back to the branch work: we had G.E.–style tank engine No.460 (L.N.E. N7), a fairly new engine built at Gorton Works in Manchester. She was a sturdy looking engine with a Westinghouse brake pump on one side of the smokebox and two big black knob-like superheater snifting valves behind the chimney. On either side of the boiler, a copper pipe ran from the smokebox into the water tanks, for use when running between King's Cross and Moorgate on the Undergroud when exhaust steam was led directly from the blast pipe into the tanks and condensed in order to reduce the amount of steam discharged in the tunnels. No.460 weighed sixty-five tons and was only a year old. Although basically of G.E. design, Gorton had hybridized her with a Great Central regulator, one of their smaller but round firehole doors and an ugly Gorton 'flowerpot' chimney.

A minute or so before we left with the 5.7pm train from Hatfield, Harry Peacock the staion foreman, came up with the train staff. Armed with this authority, lettered HATFIELD TO COLE GREEN, we set off punctually, with No.460 making light work of our fourcoach train, carrying perhaps a dozen passengers. From Hatfield to Welwyn Garden City, the branch ran alongside the main line, and then turned away eastwards across the fields towards Attimore Hall and Birchall level crossings to Cole Green, our second stop. This latter, the train crossing place on the single line, had a signalbox and two platforms. It was either the stationmaster or the signalman who met us in, took from me the train staff whilst at the same time handing over the COLE GREEN TO HERTFORD staff for the final part of our journey.

What a pretty little station Cole Green was in those days! There was a pub on the station approach, a little cluster of trees north of the station buildings, well-tended beds of flowers along the platforms and many evergreens that formed a green background, winter and summer. A mile farther on we stopped at Hertingfordbury station with its one short platform, then on over the river bridge, round to the left and up the gradient into Hertford New Station on the Wood Green to Stevenage loop line.

What had I thought of No.460? Whilst she was completely boss of the job, it did appear to me that she burnt more coal than I would have thought necessary for such a light train. Later on I learnt that Hatfield water, pumped from the underlying chalk strata, was highly charged with lime that led to the building up of thick scale on the boiler tubes. As this deposit naturally hindered the free passage of heat into the boiler water, more coal had to be burnt in order to keep up the steam pressure. Furthermore, this scale also furred up the insides of the injector delivery pipes, so much so that I saw two-inch diameter tubes so badly blocked that it was scarcely possible to push a pencil down the centre of them! Perhaps No.460's boiler was getting a bit dirty inside! But the N.7 had a roomy and comfortable cab that was as cosy as the parlour in an old-fashioned pub. And she rode as smoothly as any Rolls-Royce car. The easy-to-turn reverser wheel, with its rapid motion, was a boon and a blessing to any driver. Make no mistake about it – the old Great Eastern looked after the comfort of its enginemen.

Our diagrammed working next required us to leave the coaches at Hertford station, pick up a goods brake and depart to the Old Station on the southeastern side of the town. This took us over a short section of line where, with the flanges of the engine wheels squealing against the rails on sharp curves, we passed under overhanging trees and over narrow bridges spanning water courses. For an hour or so we shunted, before leaving for home with a dozen or so wagons hooked on the smokebox end of the engine. I forget now the reason for the rule, but tank engines working in the London suburban area always faced north; so we returned south bunker-first.

Halfway between Hertingfordbury and Cole Green we usually stopped at Holwell Sidings in order to pick up some wagons of sand from the sand-pit there. At night, perhaps under the splendour of a tranquil harvest moon, the guard went ahead to signal us along the sidings with his oil lamp. When he swung a white light from side to side, I called out "Move up" to Ernie Valentine. Each time that he checked the forward creep of the engine with a light application of the brake, air escaped with the sharp hiss so characteristic of the Westinghouse air pressure brake. At one point the engine passed alongside a sandy bank so closely that wild flowers growing on it almost brushed against my face. At length the guard waved a green light from side to side as an indication that the leading wagon was close to those loaded with sand which we had to collect. His red light stopped us and, as soon as the wagons were coupled, the guard waved his white light up and down, telling us that we could pull back.

Two activities went on in this sandpit. There was the primary one of quarrying sand, followed by filling up the excavations with London garbage. Rats of extraordinary size were said to thrive so well amongst this rubbish that some railwaymen always tied up the bottoms of their uniform trousers with string before they went in there at night, lest rats ran up their legs . . .

To me, on a perfect windless September night, with few sounds except those of the engine with its hiccupping brake pump, the night air had the scent of autumn dew on leaves close to us, or of the stubble fields across the line. Inside the cab the fire-flash lit up the polished brass fittings on the boiler faceplate, and was reflected upon the faces of the steam and other gauges. I always felt that this situation, full to the brim with steam locomotive romance, was mildly intoxicating.

The Luton and Dunstable branch, twenty and a half miles in length, was the longest and busiest of the three. It was also the most scenic and undulating in character. It, too, ran alongside the main line as far as Welwyn Garden City, before swinging away westwards through a ridge of wooded high ground. Historically, the Luton and Hertford branches began as a direct line between the two towns, but the project was disrupted by the building of the G.N.R. in 1849. The latter company bought out the smaller one, abandoned the idea of a through line and turned both ends southwards to terminals at Hatfield.

With the exception of a mile or so of double track at Luton Bute Street station, the line was divided into four single track 'Train Staff' sections for train regulation purposes. These were: Hatfield to Ayot, Ayot to Harpenden, Harpenden to Luton, and Luton West to Chaul End. At the last-named the L.M.S. single line from Dunstable to Leighton Buzzard joined our tracks end-on. Each section had its own train staff, some of which were lettered brass blocks fitted with a short steel handle, looking very much like a carpenter's mallet made in metal. The driver must always have the proper staff, although in some sections, Hatfield to Ayot for instance, if a second train was required to follow the first one, it was permitted to show the first driver the staff and then give him a written ticket that authorised him to proceed. The last train through the section carried the staff. One Hatfield driver was so conscious of the need to have the staff that he insisted it should always lie on the cab floor, under the firehole door, so that whenever he wanted to reassure himself that he had, in fact, got it, all he had to do was to glance down at it as it lay a little away from his feet. No doubt he had been concerned at some time in his career with an instance of running without a staff.

It was in mid-September, whilst firing for driver Tom Silver on the 5.49pm from King's Cross to Dunstable, that I had my introduction to the Luton branch. We had No.4301, one of the oldest of the G.N. 4–4–0s , that gave me a rough trip due to shortage of steam for the first part of the journey to Hatfield. We had taken charge of this engine at King's Cross Top Shed before going in convoy with two other light engines down through the 528 yards of the soot-encrusted Gas Works Tunnel to King's Cross station. At this date this was quite an experience for me because we arrived right in the middle of the evening rush hour, with locomotives large and small crossing and re-crossing the lines as they set back on to their various trains. Interspersed with all these busy engine movements, of course, were the smoky and noisy departures of both main line and suburban passenger trains. It was certainly a memorable scene in the heyday of steam at this London terminus.

We set off punctually with a full head of steam and a boilerful of water. I had made up the fire with plenty of coal under the firehole door before we left the Top Shed so I now took the pricker or long poker and pushed this lot of coal under the door down evenly over the firegrate in the usual way. But the hard pull up to Finsbury Park soon reduced the steam pressure and we were a few pounds down by the time we left there for our next stop at Hadley Wood. Pulling seemed hard for that old engine as she struggled along up the grades. No matter how I fire – little and often or waiting a bit – the pressure fell consistently: 160–150–145lb. It was a losing battle, during which it became painful to hear the chimney exhaust of 4301 becoming more asthmatic, whilst the slower rate of the noise from the rail joints clearly indicated that our speed was falling. What a relief it was to me when at last we topped the climb out of London a little beyond Potters Bar with scarcely more than 135 pounds of steam. No.4301 had bust my ego good and proper!

After dropping three coaches at Hatfield, off we went again all stations to Dunstable: Welwyn Garden City – Ayot – Wheathampstead – Harpenden – Luton Hoo for New Mill End – Luton – Dunstable L.M.S. Our return train, the 7.4pm from Luton, was another all-stations run, carrying very few passengers. Riding on an engine over the ups and downs along that line in the darkness of night was, at least to me as a stranger to it, a worthwhile experience. East of Luton lineside lights of any kind were few and far between, nor were there many signal lights, so it seemed as if we were careering along blindly beside shadowy shapes of lineside trees in complete blackness. One moment we were climbing and the next plunging downhill. On a road like that, too, a W class engine rolled about wildly. Then, quite unexpectedly, a faint green signal light appeared ahead. Tom shut off steam, began to apply the vacuum brake just before the dimly-lit platform at a station such as Wheathampstead began to loom up in front of us. And, of course, the train stopped in precisely its proper place for Tom as an old Hatfield hand, knew that winding and undulating road like the back of his hand.

Shortly afterwards I fired on that same 5.49pm from

King's Cross on several occasions with driver Chessum. Although we had a variety of engines – 4–4–0s Nos.3041 4301 and 4346, as well as 0–6–2T No.475 (N7) we were always rather tight for steam coming down to Hatfield. Some small consolation was, perhaps, afforded to me when I heard that about this time fireman Tom Skeggs, senior to me, had actually come to a stand short of steam with an N7 near Barnet on that same train.

Although I fired twenty-eight times for driver Chessum on a variety of engines and trains, he and I never got on too well together. Something that I had said, or did – or didn't do – had obviously upset him. One Tuesday night again with 4301 on the 5.49pm ex the Cross, whilst running between Wheathampstead and Harpenden with little better than 145lb of steam on the clock, he suddenly stepped down from his footstool, snatched the shovel out of my hands and slung half-a-dozen shovelfuls of coal up into the left hand front corner of the firegrate. All this without saying a word. He then threw the shovel back into the tender coal hole, got back behind the reversing screw and returned to driving his engine. Within a minute, however, steam pressure began to build up nicely, showing quite plainly that he certainly knew more than I did about the way to fire that old engine. I must say the incident shook me terribly!

At Luton West signalbox, the train authorisation tablet had to be picked up on the run from the signalman. He stood on the ground with an oil-lit handlamp in his hand whilst holding up the large loop with the tablet attached to it. It was the fireman's job, whilst the engine was still running at between five and eight miles an hour, to reach out of the cab with his left arm and hand which he ran through the loop. This was fair enough in daylight, but on a dark rainy night, in the uncertain glimmer of a handlamp, it was another matter altogether. On such a night I muffed my aim; the loop and its tablet went flying down below among the signal wires and point rods with a clatter. We had to stop so that I could get down and run back to the signalman who, luckily, had found the tablet and its loop by the light of his lamp. Actually, as I learned later, this was not so great a crime on my part after all, because the regulations were that all trains should stop in order to pick up the tablet.

Hatfield driver Tom Gentle, an elderly man who was gentle by nature, had a regular fireman who asked for leave on a Saturday afternoon in September 1927, so I was put in his place. We began by working a stopping passenger train from Hatfield to King's Cross with J1 0–6–0 No.3002. She steamed beautifully. On arrival we ran into No.5 platform at the 'Cross', stopping at the buffer stops end where there was a water crane leather bag hanging from the wall on our right hand side. Tom said that we must fill up here, so whilst he handed up the pipe, I went back over the coal to the tender filling hole. Now this type of flexible feed bag was liable to twist about under water pressure and a kink formed. Although I held on with all my might, the whole pipe lifted up like a wounded snake, wrenched itself free and fell down smack on to the platform, flooding it with a cascade of rushing water. Mercifully our train had carried few passengers, the last of whom had just gone past towards the ticket collector at the barrier before the flood came – otherwise there would have been trouble.

Our return working was from No.7 platform sometime between four and five o'clock with a Dunstable train. One of the station staff standing by the engine told us that we had George Bernard Shaw as a passenger. Although I knew that he lived at Ayot St. Lawrence, about four miles northwest of the Garden City, I had not at that time seen this famous author and playwright. Although I looked out on my side when we stopped at Ayot station, there was no sign of the great man among the half-dozen or so passengers who alighted on the elevated wooden-planked platform.

A sore point with Shaw, I believe, was the presence of the Blackbridge Sidings on the north side of the line between Ayot and Wheathampstead. These sidings served a huge dump for London household garbage, rather like the smaller one at Holwell on the Hertford branch. Shaw's house was not too far away, giving him cause to complain about the smoke that came from the ever-burning rubbish, as well as the unpleasant sight of loose paper and rags that were blown away and lodged in the branches of hedgerows or trees. A train-load of this rubbish came down each day from Isling-

The author with newly-delivered N7 0–6–2T No.2637, at Hatfield in 1928. *[Author's Collection]*

ton to Hatfield ready for a night run out to the sidings. Shaw, good at apt phrases, used to call the Blackbridge site, 'the local Vesuvius'.

Freight traffic was the money spinner on the Luton branch. Quite apart from wagons delivered to or collected from the goods yards at wayside stations to and from Luton, a lot of through traffic passed back to Hatfield from the busy industrial centre of Luton itself, as well as Dunstable. Whole train loads of cement came from a cement works a little west of Luton, whilst coal in quantity was also moved from Hatfield to Luton.

Once I worked for a week with an elderly driver named Arthur Robinson – known as Robbo to the other chaps. One afternoon we were on a freight turn with 0–6–0 Class B No.4169, well-liked because she was known to be a first-class steamer. Robbo was a rum sort of chap who lived in a little cottage alongside the old Great North Road by the Wrestlers pub and he had a reputation for putting young firemen in their place. On the first day, we had a few words at Dunstable but, that over and my piece said in reply, we got on all right afterwards.

Shortage of steam brought me to a complete stand once only. According to my diary this happened on Saturday 22nd October 1927 when I was with Fred Higgs driving No.913 (N7) on a morning freight from Hatfield to Luton. We stuck on the gradient in the Sherrard's Park Woods a little west of the Garden City with about 115lb of steam showing on the gauge. An old G.N. locomotive would, I feel sure, have struggled on till she was down to 100lb, but not so No.913 – in spite of all her modern features, including two splendid inside sets of Walschaerts valve gear to regulate the piston valves. "Give her a minute or two and perhaps she will come round," said Fred as we hung there on the grade. In about seven or eight minutes, with another ten pounds showing on the gauge, Fred opened the regulator, and off went the N7 – curiously enough, without a moment's hesitation.

The St. Albans branch, six and a half miles in length, ran over fairly flat and less interesting countryside. Controlled by a single train staff, it was a one-engine-in-steam line, with five stations or halts – Nast Hyde Halt, Smallford, Hill End, Salvation Army Halt and St. Albans. The line in fact extend another three-quarters of a mile to St. Albans Abbey station on the old L.N.W. section of the L.M.S., although very little traffic passed over that tail-end piece of track. A shuttle service of three-coach trains ran at about hourly intervals on weekdays over the branch and was quite popular with Hatfield housewives who liked to do their shopping in

St. Albans.

For a week in December I fired on that branch to driver Tom Addington on No.916, another N7. The trip down to the L.M.S. ran about tea-time and as we came away one dark night we both felt a jolt under the cab. All seemed in order and we carried on to our own destination, where the stationmaster told us that we had run over and killed a pig that had escaped from a porter at the Abbey station . . .

There was little freight on the branch although at the west end of Hatfield Newton there were some sidings known as the Fiddle – a name derived from that of a pub nearby. The freight service ran in the early hours before any passenger trains started. We had a very old 0–6–0, No.3101, at Hatfield and she was often booked for this duty on the St. Albans branch. Early one morning, when this engine was being driven by Jack Lawrence, a nervous chap who had come from Colwick to us at Hatfield on health grounds, an escaped inmate from the Hill End Mental Hospital, committed suicide on the line by laying his neck on the rail. Colwick Jack saw him, tried to stop 3101 but couldn't brake in the time available. Although the coroner rightly absolved Jack from all blame, it made little difference, because he worried terribly about cutting that poor man's head off.

CHAPTER NINE

Heavy Freight to London

MOST OF THE extra work that fell to the spare enginemen at Hatfield was the relief of Peterborough, New England or Hitchin men on locomotives working heavy freights, usually either coal or bricks, as they passed through on their way to Ferme Park Yard at Hornsey. The New England crews, although booked to work through to destination, were seldom able to do so, simply because their trains had either started late from the Peterborough area, or had been held up so long at signals en route. By the time they reached Hatfield, they were almost always already on overtime. Fortunate as this situation was in providing extra work and money for crews eager to get it, so far as the railway was concerned it presented a sorry picture of a transport undertaking unable to deal efficiently with the volume of traffic offered to it. Quite apart from the delays to traffic, instead of one footplate crew managing the Peterborough to London run – about 70 miles – two or even three sets of men were often necessary, and this was a most expensive arrangement altogether. Winter fogs worsened the position, leading to a situation in which the slow roads between Hitchin and London were occupied by a string of stationary freight trains.

The same thing had happened whilst I was at Grantham, with one particular exceptional case where a set of Grantham men relieved some from Colwick on the slow road at Saxondale on the Nottingham branch. They worked their day – without in fact moving – were relieved and went home to Grantham. The following day they were sent out again, relieved on the same engine – and never moved a wheel that day either! It did occur, of course, that engines locked in like that behind other trains in front, either ran out of coal or water.

The basic reason seemed to be that the marshalling yards or station sidings could not handle the amount of wagon traffic. The blockage worked back along the line, with often as many as five trains standing one immediately behind the other on the slow roads. The directors of the L.N.E.R. hardly knew what to do in order to bring about an improvement; they did, however, decide to establish Train Control Offices but this helped in a minor way only. Many traders, frustrated by the appalling length of time it took for their consignments to get through must have been driven to transfer their custom to road transport even at this early date and in my opinion a great deal of rail freight was lost for ever to the roads.

Many trips on heavy freights quite naturally came my way. The thing I liked about these trains was that they were hauled by the classy 119-ton 'Tango' 2–8–0s. With one exception, these were the biggest freight engines at work on the G.N. section of the L.N.E.R. The first of them was built as No.456 in 1913 when Gresley was trying to bring the G.N.R. up-to-date with more powerful freight engines. Locomotive-building programmes were, however, interrupted by the 1914–1918 War, but after peace came an accumulation of spare parts at Doncaster Plant was loaded up in wagons and despatched to the North British Locomotive Company at Glasgow. This firm had contracted to assemble these components into ten 2–8–0s at cost plus £700 profit on each engine. A little later on, another ten engines were built at Glasgow, at an all-in price of £9,282 each.

These early engines were, of course, all of the two-cylinder type. During the war, however, Gresley had in fact designed his first three-cylinder 2–8–0, which was ultimately built at Doncaster and numbered 461. An oddity about this engine was that Gresley used a one-off type of valve gear; two sets of outside Walschearts motion that were connected across the rear of the middle piston valve by a two-

Two-cylinder 'Tango' No.472 (not re-numbered) on an up goods train about 1924, near Marshmoor. *[Author's Collection]*

to-one arm, in a particular form that was not repeated on any other engine. Gresley was very keen on three-cylinder engines of all types, so it was hardly surprising to find that a good report followed the trials of No.461. It was claimed that she burnt almost 10 per cent less coal and used 12 per cent less water than her two-cylinder sisters. Another contract was soon placed with the N.B. Loco Co. to build ten of these three-cylinder 2–8–0s but this time with the two-to-one arm for the middle cylinder carried across the front of the cylinder block. Cost of these was £12,425 an engine. At this date, in the early 1920s, the 'tango' slow dance was popular, and enginemen named all these 2–8–0s as Tangos. Gresley might design his engines, but it was the footplatemen who handled them who gave them the colourful nicknames that are still known today . . .

I liked the three-cylinder Tangos much the best. Not only did they look more stylish, but they also pulled and sounded better altogether. There were twenty-four of them, Nos.3477-3500 (3461 being a special extra). But I loved every trip on a Tango, no matter whether it was a two or a three-cylinder one. Like the 2–6–0 Gresley Ragtimes, the Tangos had something about them that was so typical of the Great Northern locomotive renaissance engineered by that great engineer. The whole fleet of forty-five Tangos was shedded at New England, Peterborough, for their duties at that time were confined to working 80-wagon trains between there and London.

George Harrington, a slightly-built, tallish and quiet-tempered man, was the driver on my first Tango trip. Late one afternoon, we relieved a Peterborough crew on two-cylinder No.3474 working 80-wagons of coal bound for Ferme Park Yard. We climbed up into the cab as she stood at the outer home signals near Sherriff's Mill on the north side of Hatfield. I remember I looked at the huge boiler perched over the four pairs of 4′8″ coupled driving wheels and thought what a massive engine this was.

As soon as we got under way and pulled away towards the station, No.3474 banged and bumped in a real hard-hitting style. The cavernous coughs of the chimney exhaust, heard through the firehole door as I bent down shovelling coal into the firebox, tossed walnut-sized pieces of red-hot coal above the firebed like so many bouncing ping-pong balls. This particular engine rode rather rough, too, accompanied with a lot of banging and bashing of metal parts as if a blacksmith was aboard with us hammering hard on iron. But 3474 steamed splendidly as she tangoed her heavy train of coal round the curve up to Marshmoor and on to Brookmans Park. The exhaust injector (partly operated by exhaust steam led back from the blast pipe in the smokebox) worked well, sending a steady supply of water into the boiler.

We kept to the slow road on the east side of the main line all the way up to Potters Bar. The Great Northern, when it added tracks about the turn of the century, placed the slow goods roads on either side of the original tracks, leaving fast lines in the middle. Halfway between Brookmans Park and Potters Bar, standing lonely and obsolete on the east side embankment, was the stone coal-tax pillar indicating the northern boundary of the Metropolitan area. Formerly, a tax was levied on every ton of coal that went past this pillar into the Metropolis. George pointed this obelisk out to me that afternoon and whenever afterwards I passed here in daylight, I always glanced at this old mark.

"I fancy we shall stand here until the evening suburban passenger service rush is over," said George as we came to a stand at Potters Bar home signal. "Will you go to the box and carry out Rule 55?" That meant I had to walk over to the signalman on the other side of the main line, remind him that our train was standing at his signal, see that he put a locking collar on the relevant lever, and then return to my driver. This well-known rule, one of the most important for all enginemen, was intended to prevent a signalman from forgetting a standing train and allowing another to run into it from the rear.

An hour or so later, about 7.0pm we set off again, our 2–8–0 working really hard at the outset in order to get the heavy train onto the main line. This was followed by a careful creep downhill into Potters Bar Tunnel which at that date had only two roads through it. When it was taken into account that we had eighty laden wagons behind us, none of them fitted with an automatic brake, it will be appreciated how careful a driver had to be going downhill in order to ensure that the weight of the train did not push him along beyond the brake power on the engine into a run-away. As we slipped down towards the tunnel mouth, George made constant but light applications of the vacuum brake, keeping our speed down to a controllable rate.

We entered the tunnel with a light clear-burning fire that gave out only a little smoke. Looking back over the coal on the tender, I could see how the firelight lit up the regular pattern of the brickwork on the arched roof of the tunnel, thickly encrusted with old soot. As No. 3474 coasted downhill in the close confines of that tunnel, she went along with the BUMP-BANG-BUMP so typical of all two-cylinder Tangos. More than any other engine, they suffered badly from G.N. motion knocks and it was probably this that helped give them their nickname. But how marvellous it was to be on the footplate of this large and purposeful locomotive, hauling 800 tons of coal up to London!

After passing New Barnet, the signals increased in frequency and in complexity to such an extent that it seemed I should be a long time before I learnt them all and could be any real help to drivers. There were times when I could guess that the green light on the left side applied to us, but in many instances there were three or four signal lights in a row and I had no idea which of them related to the particular track that we were on. As yet there were few colour light signals on the line, the majority still being plain semaphores with oil-lit lamps. Ferme Park Yard, when we arrived, looked brimful with wagons of coal, but an empty siding was soon found for us to leave our 80. No. 3474 was taken into Hornsey shed, where George and I were instructed by the Running Foreman to travel back to Hatfield as passengers on the next available train.

All of the eleven three-cylinder Tangos which I fired combined good pulling with easy steaming. One of this type usually worked the 80-wagon brick train from the Yaxley or Fletton brickyards to London daily, numbered 107 Up in the working timetables. On the G.N. Section, down trains had even numbers whilst the up ones had odd numbers. My first brick train run however, was on 265 Up

2–8–2 'Booster' No.2393 on one of the hundred-wagon trains in the early 1930s. Some freight engine! The pipe under the cab side carried the exhaust from the booster engine to the smokebox. [Author's Collection]

Three-cylinder 'Tango' 2–8–0 No.3499 on a coal train heading for Ferme Park. This particular engine is fitted with an experimental top feed for injector water. [Author's Collection]

Cole Green station, photographed in 1972.
[Author's Collection]

Relics: fireman's dinner box, shovel, water gauge lamp and footplate handbrush.
[Author's Collection]

during a cold damp misty afternoon in November 1927 with driver Bill Chessum. Three-cylinder No. 3498 started her heavy load away from Hatfield in fine style with never a falter in the one-two-three pulsations of her pistons as they got the 1250-ton gross load on the move. The sound of steel upon steel as the blade of my shovel slid across the protector plate along the bottom of the firehole door opening rang out as I aimed coal evenly over the long, narrow firebed. As that big engine plodded steadily southwards, eating up coal with a healthy appetite, the steam gauge needle held as steady as a rock. Whilst the exhaust injector on my side sang as it squirted replenishment water into the boiler, I sat down on my tiny wooden seat fixed to the cab side, listening with fascination to the deep powerful chuff-chivvy-chuff exhaust beats of 3498.

In Potters Bar Tunnel, with steam shut off, the coasting note of No. 3498 was a soothing hip-pet-tey-hop, repeated over and over again as her three massive brass-bushed big ends thumped against their steel crankpins.

At the end of our run an odd thing happened as we stood in front of the long signal gantry at the north end of Hornsey station. The mist had thickened a little to fog, although it was not that bad. Another express freight, hauled by one of the new 2–6–0 K3 class, came to a stand alongside us at the signals. The driver was sitting on his seat whilst his fireman busied himself putting away tools in readiness for the time when he would be relieved. Driver Chessum turned in his seat, "How are you?", he shouted over to the other driver after a few moments, "Anything wrong?" "No, we are just waiting for the signal," called back the chap. "Well, it's your signal that's off. You are on the Up Slow!" shouted back Bill. The other driver jumped off his seat, quickly crossed over and stared up at the signals; and as quickly nipped back to tug at his regulator handle. "Thanks," he shouted back with a wave, "I thought I was still on the main. I forgot we had been turned to the Slow further back!" He was obviously a Kings Cross driver, well acquainted with the signals on his own stamping ground, but he had got misled on his own doorstep.

In between Tango turns, I also had outings on the durable and dependable G.C. 2–8–0 R.O.D.s. Strangely enough, too, there were still one or two of the ancient 0–8–0 'Long Toms' of G.N. design still creeping up to London on minor freight trains in my day. Fitting staff, however, had begun to lose interest in these old warriors, so that they were getting into a rough condition. I remember they set up an awful clatter in their side rods when driven at all fast as light engines. One morning I fired on a new engine, K3 class No.207, on her way up to Kings Cross. Engines of this mixed traffic class were not one of Gresley's biggest successes. They pulled all right, it is true, but they rode as rough as any, so much so in fact that enginemen called them Jazzers. A carrying pair of wheels under their cabs was what they needed.

No.207, it may be added, like some of the new N7 class, had left-hand drive that put the fireman over on the right, with the need to fire left-handed.

Saturday 26th November 1927 was a date for me to remember, for I had the good fortune to find myself on No.2393, one of the two special 2–8–2 or P1 Mikado heavy freight locomotives. It was a foggy afternoon and I was with driver Bill Chessum again. After signing on 4.0pm Control Relief, the Running Foreman sent us passengers to Welwyn Garden City in order to relieve New England men on an up coal train, held by signals at that station. The fog was so thick that, as we walked down to the signal gantry, I could hear steam hissing gently from an engine's waste water cocks before I could actually see her. Soon one headlamp and then a huge black shape loomed up in the gathering darkness.

No.2393 and her sister engine No.2394, weighing 151 tons apiece, were built in 1925 at Doncaster and the first of the pair was shown at the Railway Centenary Celebrations held at Darlington that year, where I first saw her. The story behind their construction is that Gresley was able to persuade the Directors of the L.N.E.R. to let him build these two engines for experiments in the handling of the heavy trains between Wath Yard in Yorkshire and the coal exporting port of Immingham, as well as on the Peterborough – London coal trains. I do not know whether either engine ever saw Wath Yard but both were soon stabled at New England shed with the job of handling 100-wagon trains up to Ferme Park – working up one day and back down the next. No.2393 was fitted with a booster engine as an auxiliary power unit under her cab for help in starting and perhaps on gradients too. One could say that these Mikados were to a large extent copies of the Gresley Pacifics, with boilers and three-cylinder motion almost identical. Instead, however, of the six 6′8″ driving wheels of the express passenger class, the Mikados had 5′2″ diameter driving wheels. In my opinion, these two Mikados were the best-looking of all the Gresley locomotives. The four smaller driving wheels went better with the long boilers than the three larger wheels on the Pacifics. On the freight side, the nickname of Boosters became the commonplace identification among enginemen when referring to 2393 or 2394.

A specially arranged coal train, the 9.15am New England to Ferme Park, listed as 327 Up coal, Class 'C', the only 100-wagon train in the main line timetable, was the province of these monster engines. A train of this size, carrying a thousand tons of coal and approximately 670 yards in length, was an outsize one among the general run of 80-wagoners which, truth to tell, really fitted better into the signalling and length limits on some sections of that main line. The Operating Department, in fact, were never particularly enthusiastic about this very long 100-wagon train.

In the usual run of things, the Booster and its train passed through Hatfield between 3 and 4pm. What a stirring sight it was to see the huge 2–8–2 coming up the grade at a steady twenty miles an hour, with a great twisting column of blackish smoke rising up from her stubby but noble chimney. Even the hard-of-hearing had no difficulty in picking up the majestic thunder of the exhaust as she pitted her three sliding pistons against the 1,600 tons gross load hooked to her tender. The distant sound of that engine climbing up to Red Hall could be heard right on the other side of Hatfield Park, where I listened to it several times when off duty.

Coming back to my own trip; the New England driver told Bill that the booster itself, a two-cylinder simple engine under the cab, was out of order and isolated that night. In consequence we had eighty wagons only as our load. As we sat in the comfortable cab, other trains passed us, both up and down, till about 7.0pm when the light of our up slow road signal turned to green. No.2393 pulled away superbly. As we approached the Welwyn Garden City signalbox, it was my duty to watch whether the signalman gave us a green light from his handlamp to indicate whether there were any other freight trains in the permissive block section up to Hatfield. This was something highly probable on that foggy Saturday evening and, since a driver was permitted to enter such sections and proceed as far as the line was clear, it was important for him to know, at night or in fog, when he was likely to come up against the brake van of the last one let in. Signalmen, whilst holding the green handlamp signal outside their box windows, would hold up the other hand and extend one, two, three, four or even five fingers to tell us; one in, two in, and so on. However, there was no such signal that night and Bill opened out No.2393 with confidence southwards towards Hatfield. When we got there, instead of being held at signals again, as we had expected, to our surprise we were turned out on to the up main line. What a chance this was for Bill to let No.2393 show her paces – and did she grasp the opportunity! Only 80 wagons, I know, but she could pull, and run, and steam, like a real thorough-bred. Gone, too, were the bumps and bangs of a Tango! We had a real rousing run up through Hatfield, Red Hall, Marshmoor, Brookmans Park to Potters Bar and straight on through the tunnels to New Barnet. It was sheer pleasure to ride on an engine in which free steaming and ample power were so happily wedded! No.2393 presented me with the most memorable of all my freight trips . . .

No further P1 class were ever built, but I don't know why. Perhaps they should have used them on 80-wagon trains worked at higher speeds – although in those days of coal wagons without continuous brakes, they were before their time. However, both engines carried on until World War II, during which they were scrapped at a time when railwaymen saw new 2–10–0 locomotives coming out to help us win the war. I doubt if they were as good as Gresley's 1925 Mikados.

On 19th January 1928 came my footplate farewell; I signed on at 5.45am, knowing that this would be my last day on the footplate. Sad to say, my eyes had been giving me some trouble and at Moorfields Eye Hospital in London I had been told that I must henceforward wear glasses. The railway practice at that time was that no engineman might wear these; so as a result I was off the footplate.

On that final day I was with George Harrington on two-cylinder Tango No.3476 working a train of mixed goods and coal up to Ferme Park Yard. It was a fine winter's day as we moved from signal to signal in the same leisurely way as had happened so many times before. About midday we arrived at the Hornsey North up signal gantry, where after a short while a pair of Hornsey men relieved us.

When I stepped down from the cab of that Tango, with 211 firing turns to my credit, sadly enough my days on the footplate had finished. But I walked away from No.3476 carrying with me a wealth of happy memories of those gloriously impressive days working with steam locomotives on the old London & North Eastern Railway.

books from

D. BRADFORD BARTON LTD

Great Western Steam in Action edited by L.M. Collins
Great Western Steam in Action: 2 edited by L.M. Collins
Great Western Steam in Action: 3 edited by L.M. Collins
Great Western Steam in Action: 4 edited by L.M. Collins
Great Western Steam in Action: 5 edited by L.M. Collins
Great Western Steam in Action: 6 edited by L.M. Collins
Great Western Steam in Action: 7 edited by L.M. Collins
Great Western Steam through the Years: 1 Tony Fairclough & Alan Wills
Great Western Steam through the Years: 2 Tony Fairclough & Alan Wills
Great Western Branch Line Steam: 1 edited by C.L. Williams
Great Western Branch Line Steam: 2 edited by C.L. Williams
Great Western Steam Miscellany: 1 edited by C.L. Williams
Great Western Steam Miscellany: 2 edited by C.L. Williams
Great Western Steam in the West Country edited by '4588'
Great Western Steam on Shed edited by C.L. Williams
More Great Western Steam on Shed edited by C.L. Williams
Great Western Steam in Close Up edited by P.W.B. Semmens
Great Western Steam at Swindon Works Brian Morrison
Great Western Steam Preserved edited by Grenville R. Hounsell
Great Western Steam South of the Severn R.E. Toop
Great Western Steam in Cornwall B.A. Butt & Tony Fairclough
More Great Western Steam in Cornwall Tony Fairclough
Great Western Steam in Devon edited by Tony Fairclough
More Great Western Steam in Devon Tony Fairclough & Alan Wills
Great Western Steam off the Beaten Track G.F. Bannister
Great Western Steam in South Wales S. Rickard
More Great Western Steam in South Wales S. Rickard
Great Western Steam in the Midlands Michael Mensing
Great Western Steam Doubleheaded edited by C.L. Williams
More Great Western Steam Doubleheaded edited by do.
Great Western Steam in Wales & the Border Counties edited by C.L. Williams
More Great Western Steam in Wales & the Border Counties edited by C.L. Williams
Great Western Steam through the Cotswolds C.L. Williams
Great Western Steam around Bristol edited by C.L. Williams
The last decade of Great Western Main Line Steam T.E. Williams
GWR Service Timetable Appendices 1945

London Midland Steam in Action edited by W. Askew Blake
London Midland Steam in Action: 2 edited by W. Askew Blake
London Midland Steam in Action: 3 edited by W. Askew Blake
London Midland Steam in Action: 4 edited by W. Askew Blake
London Midland Steam Locomotives: 1 Brian Morrison
London Midland Steam Locomotives: 2 Brian Morrison
London Midland Steam from Lineside Brian Morrison
London Midland Steam in the Midlands Michael Mensing
London Midland Steam Over Shap Derek Cross
London Midland Steam in the Northern Fells Derek Cross
London Midland Steam North of the Border Derek Cross
London Midland Steam in North Wales W.G. Rear
London Midland Steam Doubleheaded edited by W. Askew Blake
London Midland Steam in the East Midlands J.F. Henton
London Midland Steam on the ex-L&Y edited by R.S. Greenwood
London Midland Steam on Shed compiled by '45562'
London Midland Steam: Skipton to Carlisle R.H. Leslie

London Midland Steam in Yorkshire P. Cookson
London Midland Steam in the North West J.R. Carter
More London Midland Steam in the North West N. Dyckhoff
London Midland Steam in the Peak District J.R. Hillier
London Midland Steam around Carlisle R.H. Leslie
LMSR Steam 1923-1948 H.C. Casserley
LMSR Locomotives 1923-1948: 1 H.C. Casserley
LMSR Locomotives 1923-1948: 2 H.C. Casserley
LMSR Locomotives 1923-1948: 3 H.C. Casserley
(de-luxe available of above 4 vols)
LNWR Locomotives of C.J. Bowen Cooke O.S. Nock
Class 8F Stanier 2-8-0s Stanier 8F Loco Society

Southern Steam in Action: 1 Tony Fairclough & Alan Wills
Southern Steam in Action: 2 Tony Fairclough & Alan Wills
Southern Steam in Action: 3 Tony Fairclough & Alan Wills
Southern Steam in Action: 4 Tony Fairclough & Alan Wills
Southern Steam 1923-1939 John L. Smith
Southern Steam from Lineside Derek Cross
Southern Steam South and East Stanley Creer
More Southern Steam South and East Stanley Creer
Southern Steam South and West Tony Fairclough & Alan Wills
More Southern Steam South and West Tony Fairclough & Alan Wills
Southern Steam on the Isle of Wight Tony Fairclough & Alan Wills
Southern Steam on Shed Tony Fairclough & Alan Wills
More Southern Steam on Shed Tony Fairclough & Alan Wills
Southern Steam Locomotive Survey:
1: **early Maunsell classes** Tony Fairclough & Alan Wills
2: **later Maunsell classes** Tony Fairclough & Alan Wills
3: **Merchant Navy Pacifics** Tony Fairclough & Alan Wills
4: **Bulleid Light Pacifics** Tony Fairclough & Alan Wills
5: **Urie classes** Tony Fairclough & Alan Wills
6: **Drummond classes** Tony Fairclough & Alan Wills
7: **Adams classes** Tony Fairclough & Alan Wills
8: **Wainwright classes** Tony Fairclough & Alan Wills
Southern Steam Doubleheaded Tony Fairclough & Alan Wills
Southern Steam in the West Country Tony Fairclough & Alan Wills
More Southern Steam in the West Country Tony Fairclough & Alan Wills
Southern Electrics edited by B.W. Rayner
Southern Branch Line Steam: 1 Tony Fairclough & Alan Wills
Southern Branch Line Steam: 2 Tony Fairclough & Alan Wills
Southern Steam through the Years Tony Fairclough & Alan Wills
Steam on the Brighton Line edited by A.C. Perryman
Recollections of the Southern Between the Wars H.C. Casserley
Bodmin & Wadebridge Railway Tony Fairclough & Alan Wills
Southern Steam in Works Tony Fairclough & Alan Wills
Southern Steam in Close Up Tony Fairclough & Alan Wills
SR Working Timetable Appendices 1934

North Eastern Steam in Action Brian Morrison
North Eastern Steam from Lineside P.J. Lynch
North Eastern Steam in Northumbria Malcolm Dunnett
North Eastern Pacifics Norman E. Preedy
North Eastern Steam Locomotive Album P.J. Lynch
LNER Locomotives 1923-1948 H.C. Casserley
LNER Steam 1923-1948 H.C. Casserley

BR Diesels in Action edited by G. Weekes
BR Diesels in Action: 2 edited by G. Weekes
BR Diesels in Action: 3 edited by G. Weekes
BR Diesels in Action: 4 edited by G. Weekes

BR Diesels in Action: 5 edited by G. Weekes
BR Diesels on Shed N.E. Preedy
BR Diesels in Close-Up N.E. Preedy & H.L. Ford
BR Diesels in the Landscape Derek Cross
WR Diesel-Hydraulics Norman E. Preedy & G.F. Gillham
BR Diesels and Electrics around Britain A.W. Hobson
BR Diesels Doubleheaded edited by G. Weekes
Diesels in London and the Home Counties P.A. Dobson
Diesels on Eastern Region edited by Norman E. Preedy
Diesels on Western Region edited by H.L. Ford
Diesels on Scottish Region S. Rickard
Diesels on Midland Region edited by G. Weekes
Diesels in the Highlands edited by G. Weekes
Diesels in the West Midlands and Central Wales G.F. Bannister
Diesels on Cornwall's Main Line H.L. Ford
Diesels on the Devon Main Line edited by H.L. Ford
Modern Rail Album A.W. Hobson
Branch Lines Round Britain in the Diesel Era J.A.M. Vaughan
DMUs Countrywide P.J. Fowler
The Westerns: BR Class 52 Diesel-Hydraulics H.L. Ford
The Warships: BR Class 42/43 Diesel-Hydraulics H.L. Ford
BR Diesel Miscellany: 1 edited by G. Weekes
BR Diesels in Detail M. Oakley & Brian Morrison
Diesels West G.F. Gillham

BR Standard Steam in Action Derek Cross
BR Standard 2-10-0 Class 9F edited by G. Weekes
BR Standard Steam in Close-Up Tony Fairclough & Alan Wills
BR Standard Britannia Pacifics edited by G. Weekes
Memories of Steam around Britain P.J. Lynch
Scottish Steam in the 1920s R.D. Stephen
Scottish Steam Miscellany R.D. Stephen
Scottish Branch Line Steam edited by Jack Kernahan
Scottish Main Line Steam edited by Jack Kernahan
Steam in the Western Highlands edited by Jack Kernahan
Last Decade of Scottish Steam Derek Cross
Steam on the Waverley Route R.H. Leslie
Steam on Britain's Miniature Railways Robin Butterell
Steam on the Somerset & Dorset G.A. Richardson
Steam around Britain in the Seventies L.A. Nixon
Cornwall's Railways A. Fairclough
The Railways of Devon A. Kingdom
Specials in Action A.R. Butcher
Mineral Railways of the West Country Tony Fairclough
Industrial Steam Adrian J. Booth
British Steam around the Regions K.R. Pirt & D.E. Penney
The Tralee & Dingle Railway David G. Rowlands
European Narrow Gauge Steam: 1 D. Trevor Rowe
European Narrow Gauge Steam: 2 D. Trevor Rowe
Industrial Narrow Gauge Railways in Britain P.D. Nicholson
British Narrow Gauge Steam edited by Michael J. Messenger
More British Narrow Gauge Steam Michael J. Messenger
Steam on the SNCF Peter F. Winding
European Steam in Action P.J. Lynch
Austrian Steam from Lineside V.C.K. Allen
Portuguese Steam from Lineside V.C.K. Allen
Railways of the Republic of Ireland 1925-1975 M.H.C. Baker
Articulated Locomotives of the World Donald Binns
South American Steam M.H.J. Finch
Steam in India Hugh Hughes
Steam in the Andes Brian Fawcett
New Zealand Steam Spectacular Derek Cross
British-Built Steam Locomotives Overseas J.N. Westwood
Vulcan Foundry Locomotives 1832-1956 D.E. Gudgin
Electric Locomotives of the World F.J.G. Haut